101
Relaxing
Landscapes
Coloring Book

THIS BOOK BELONGS TO:

____

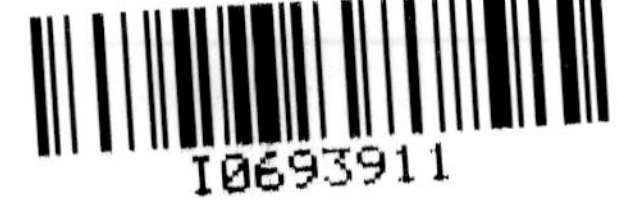

TEST COLOR PAGES

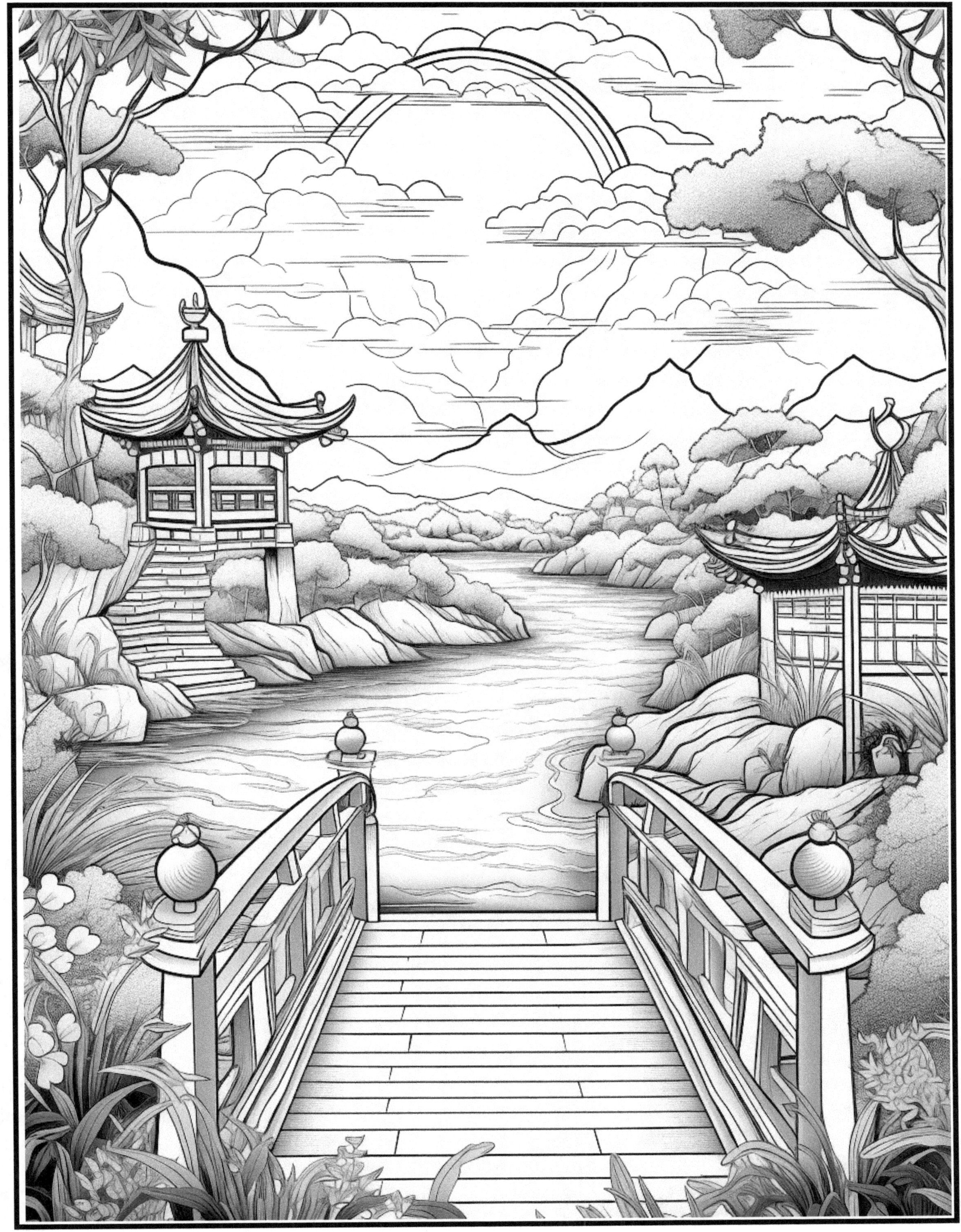

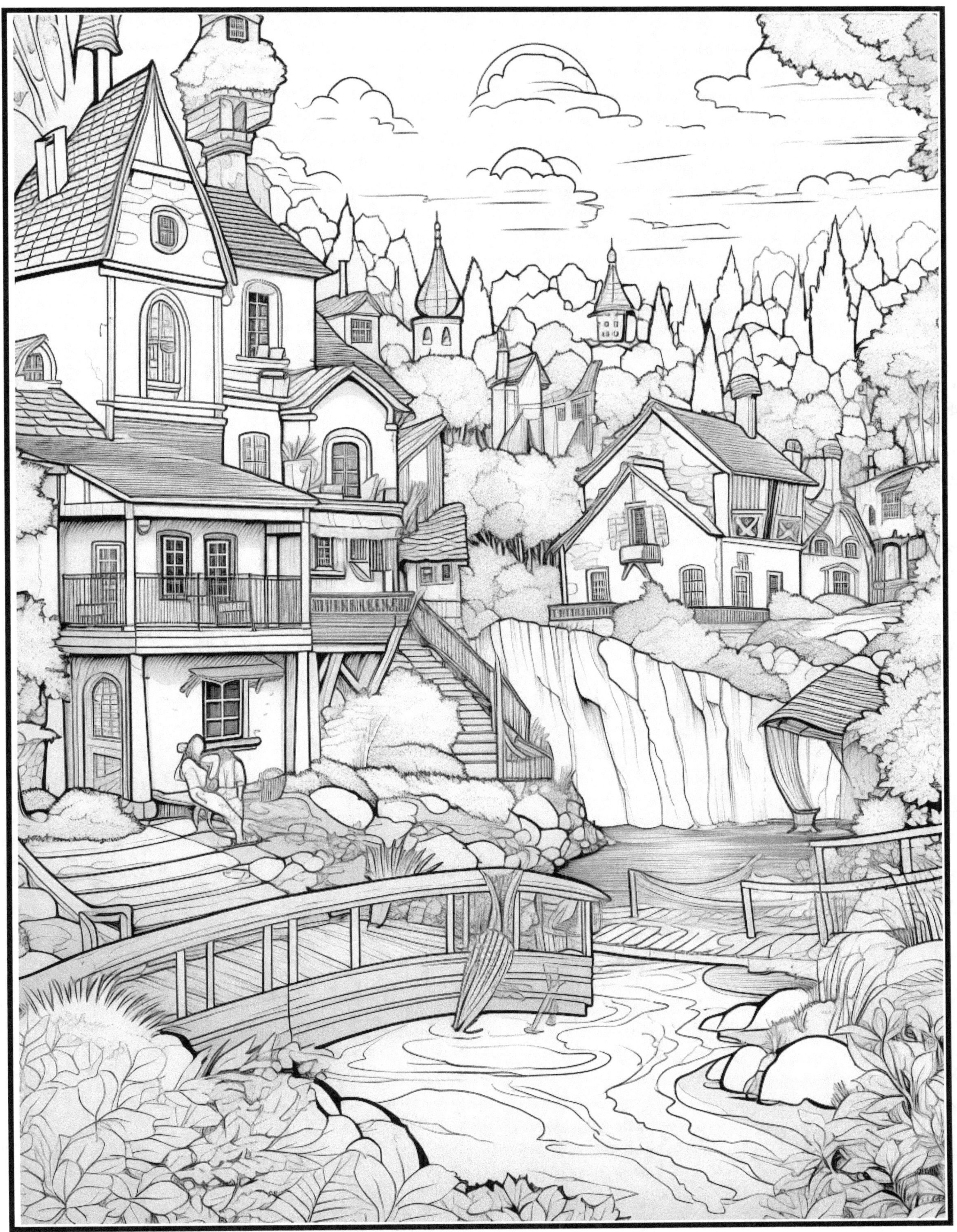

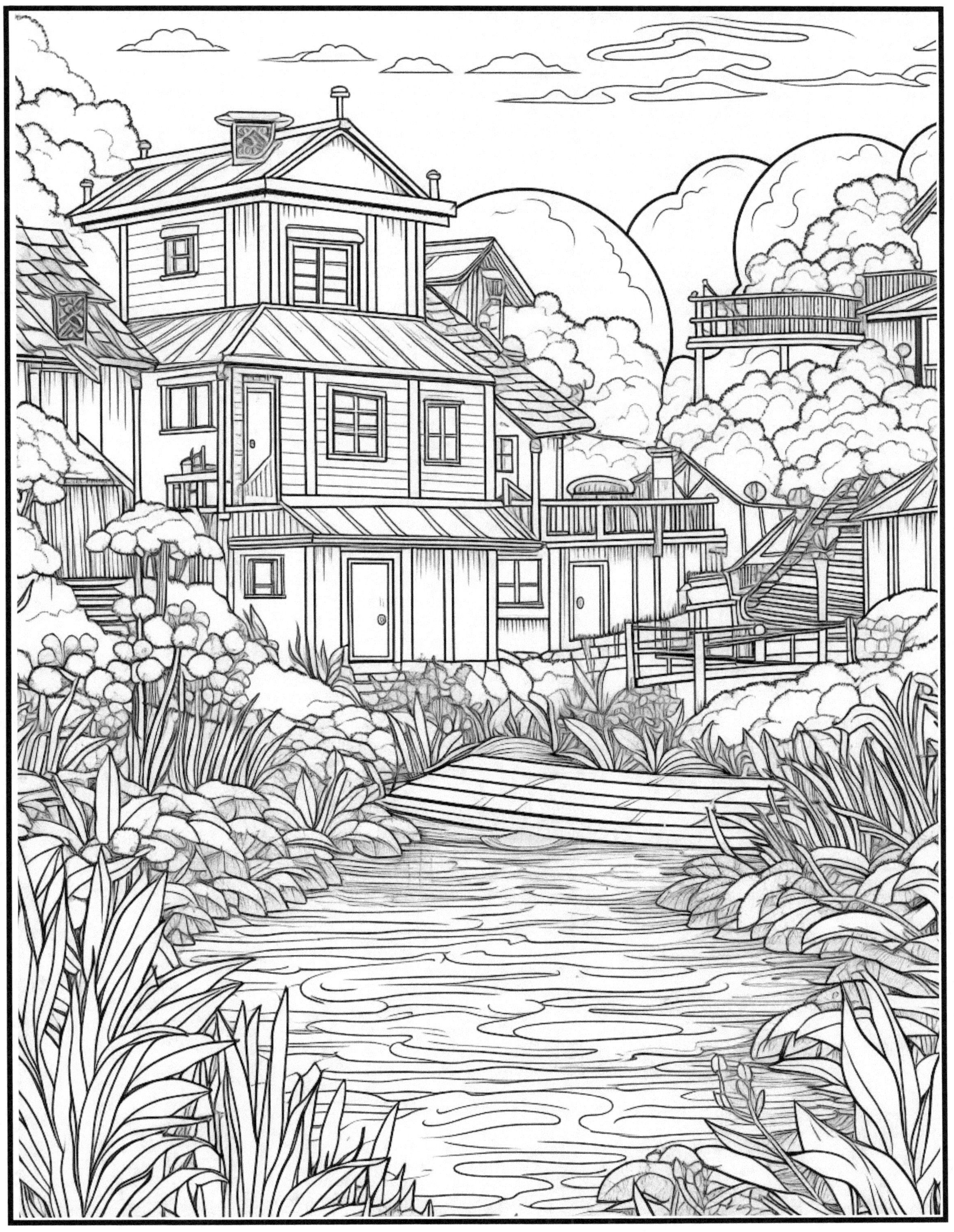

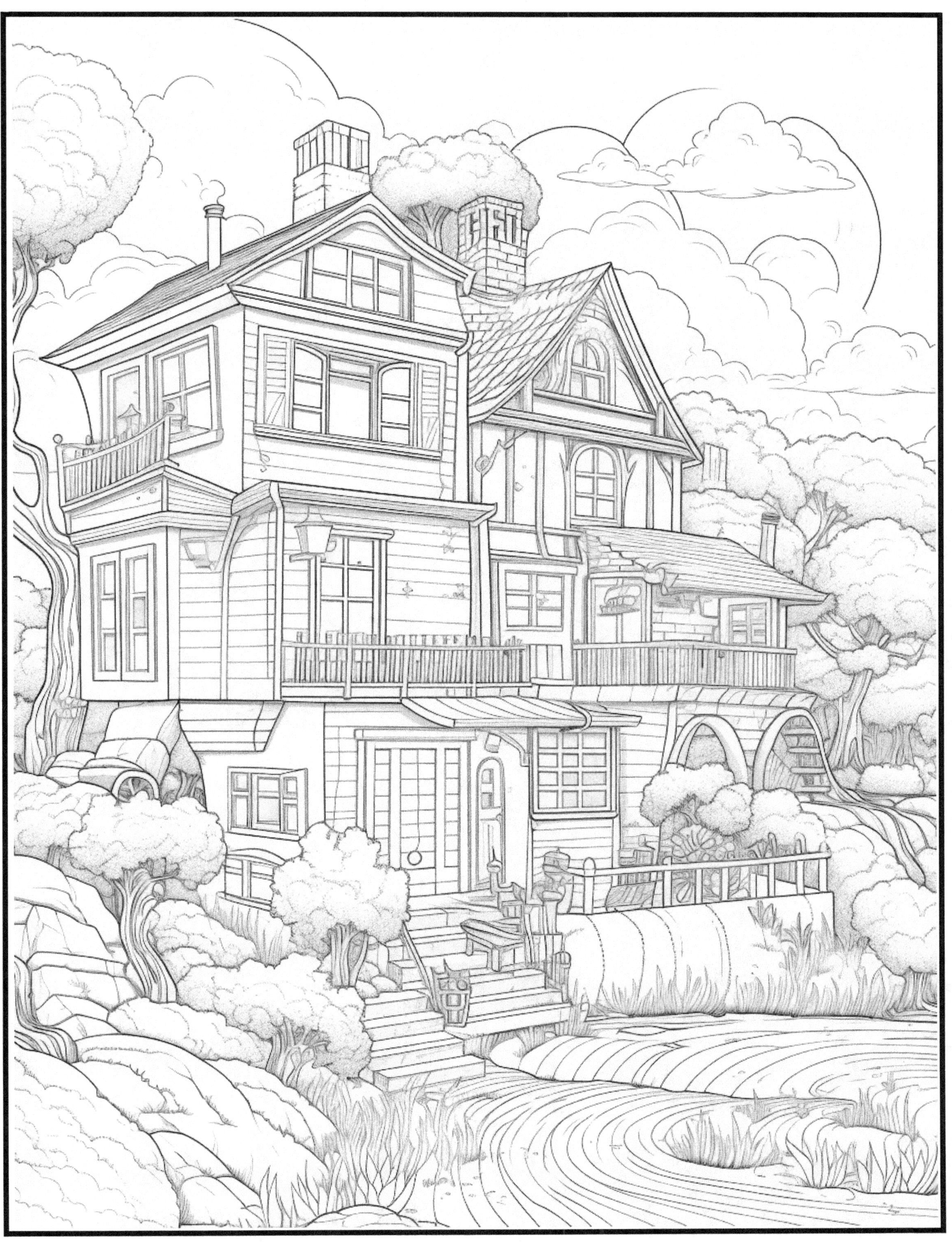

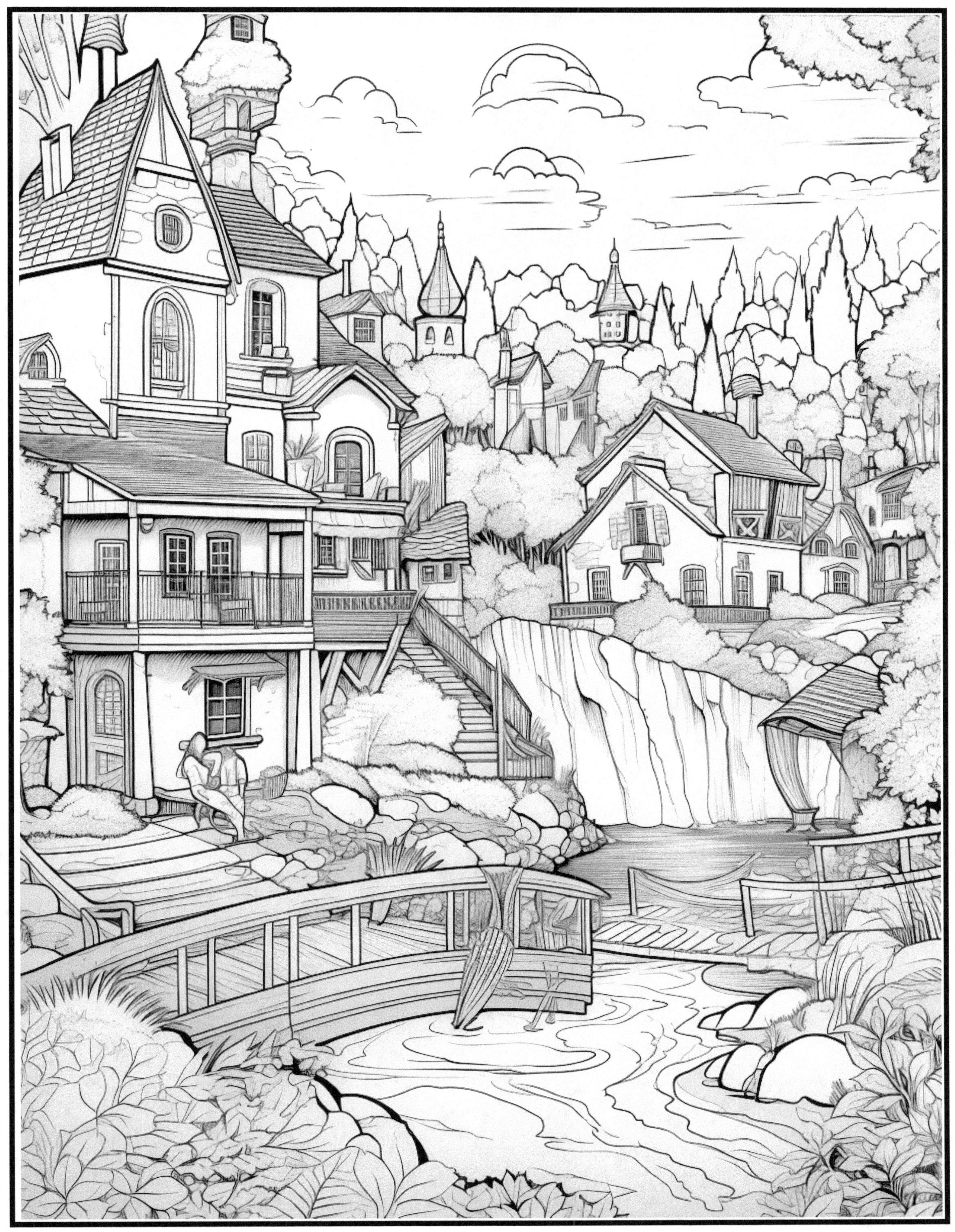

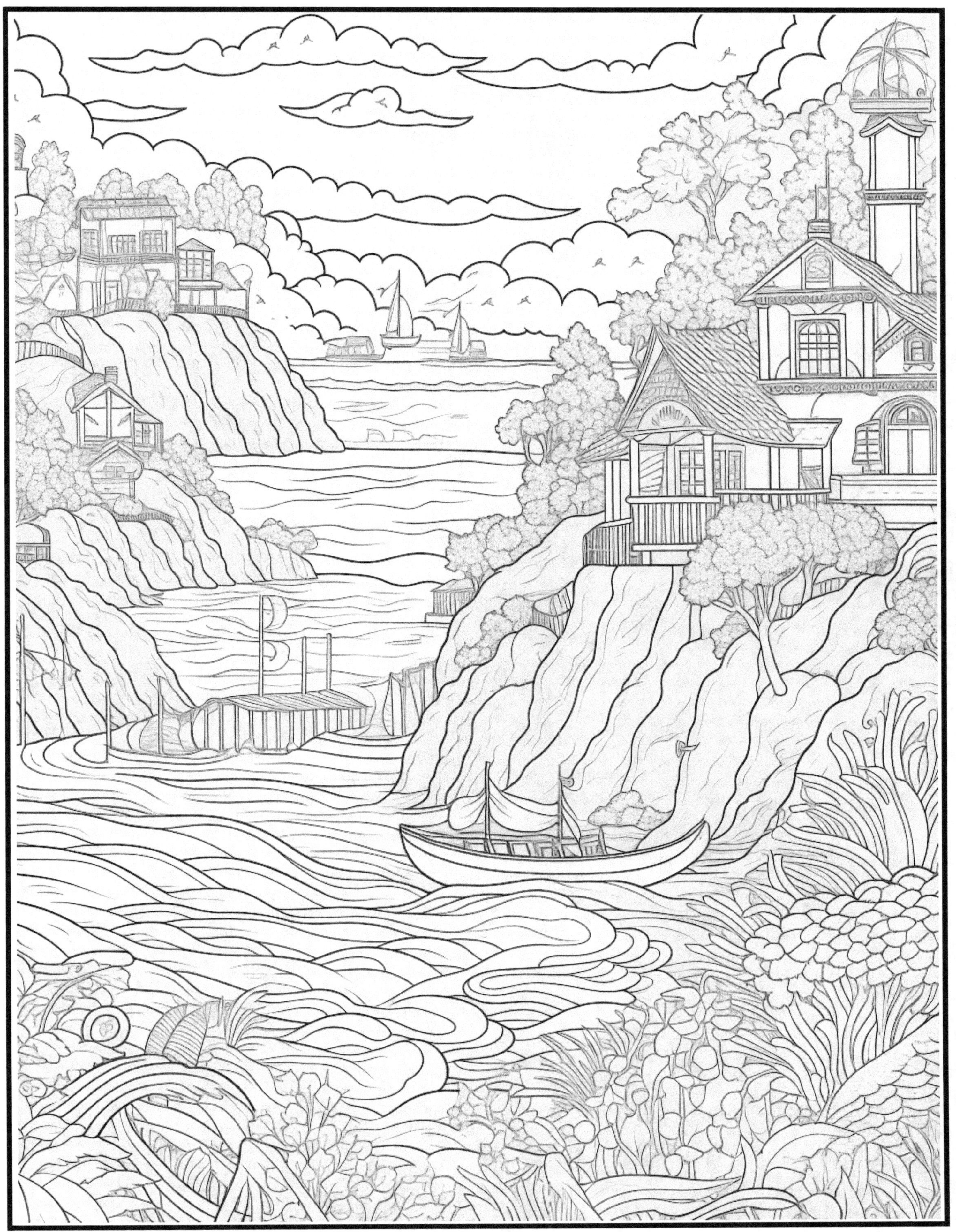

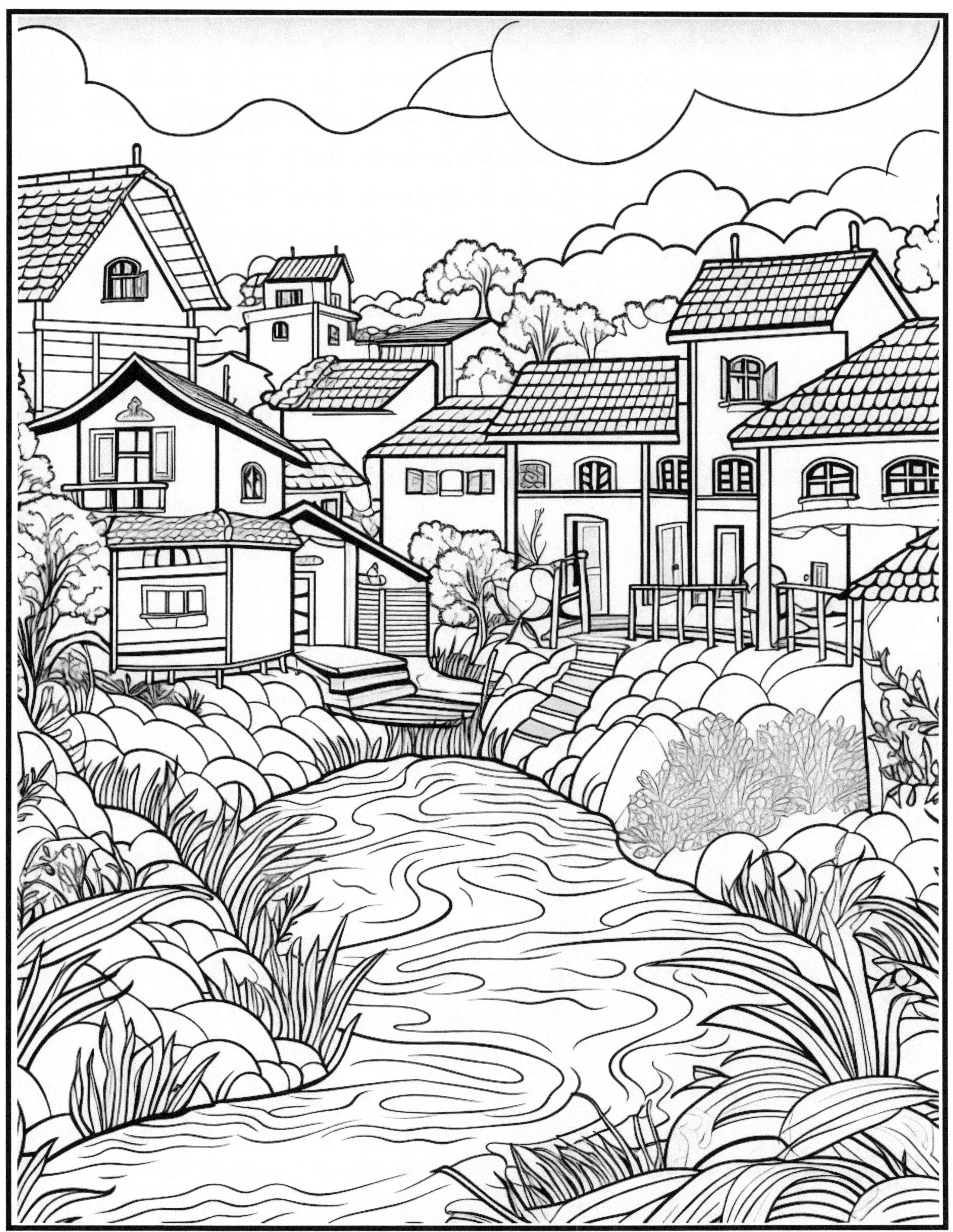

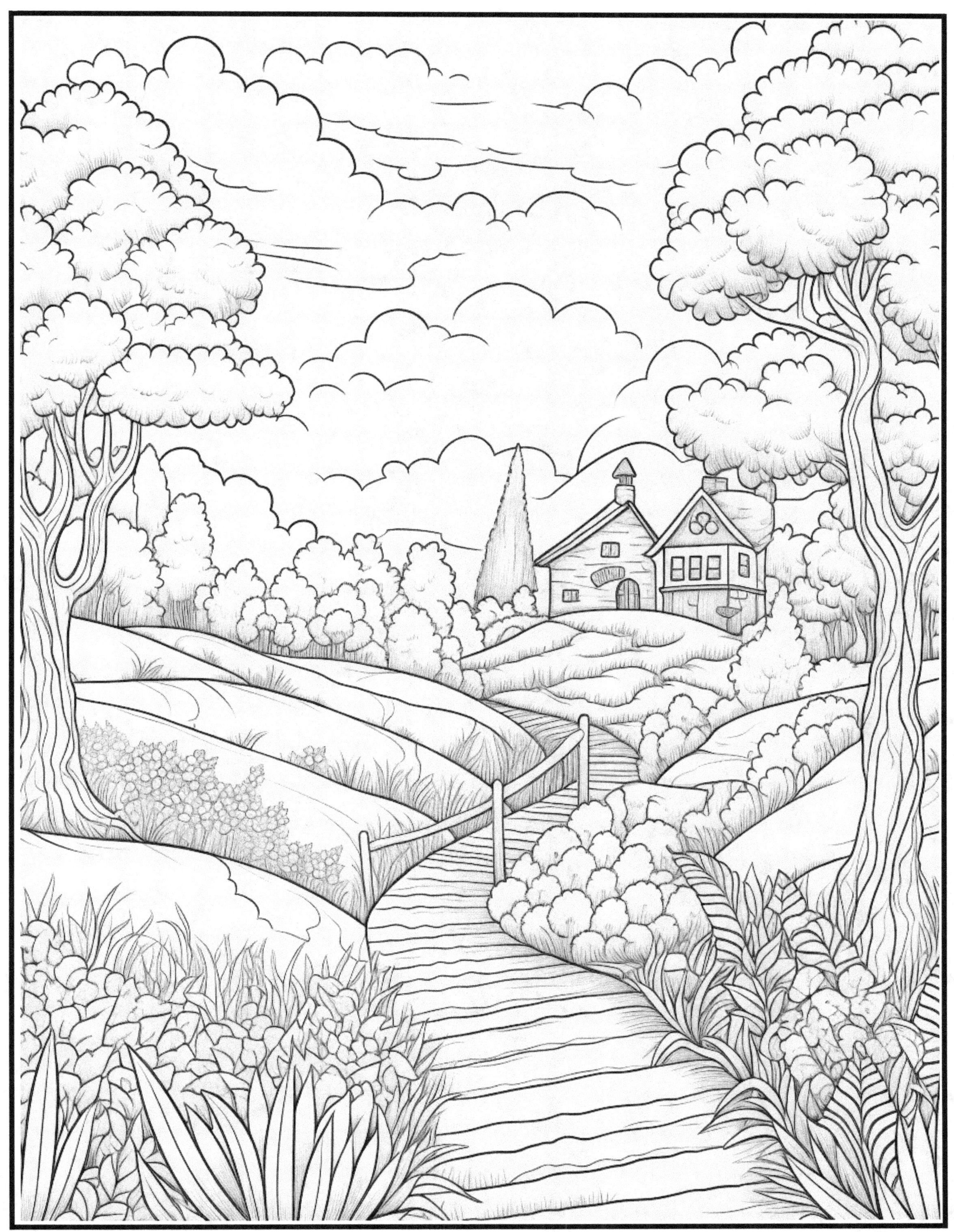

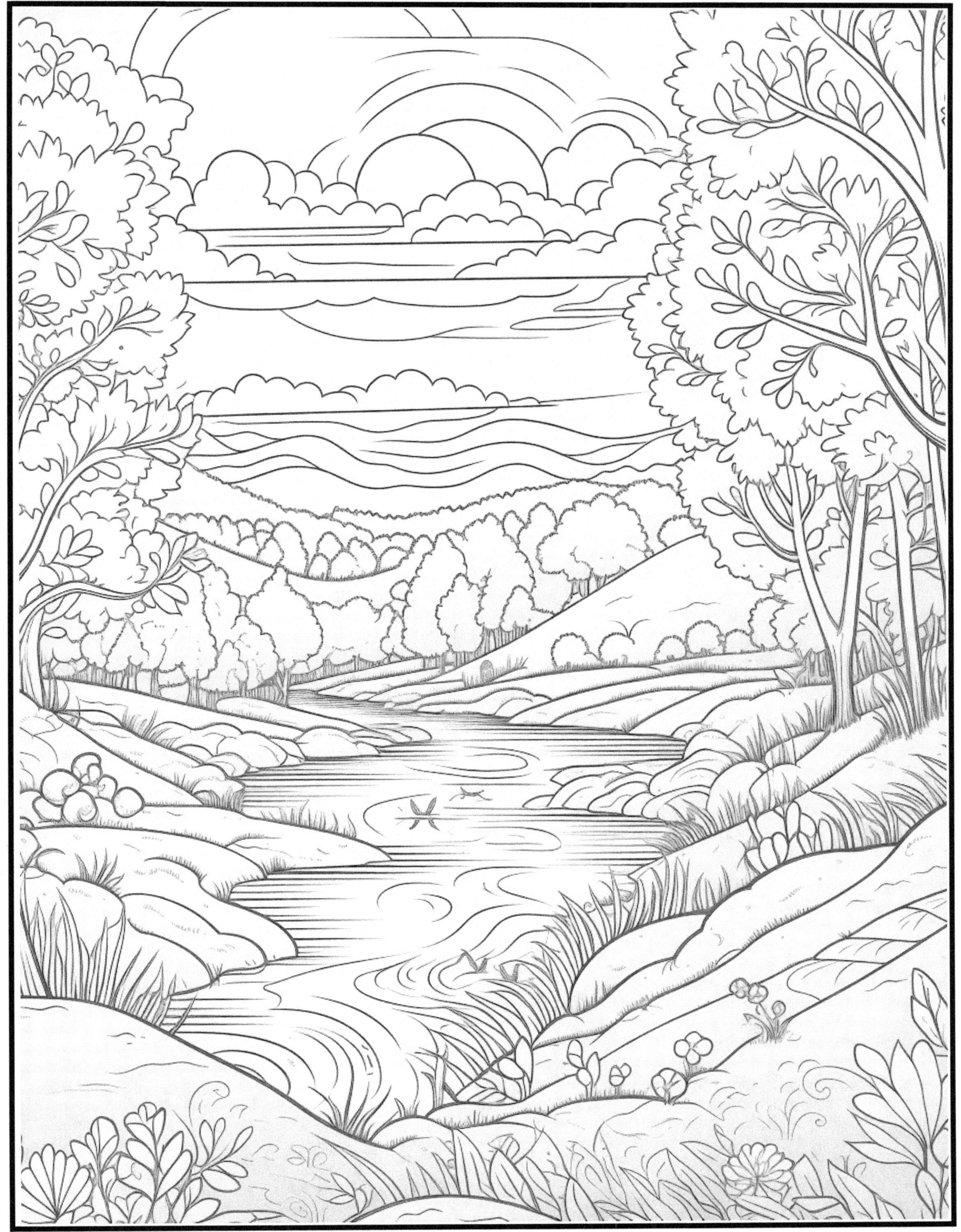

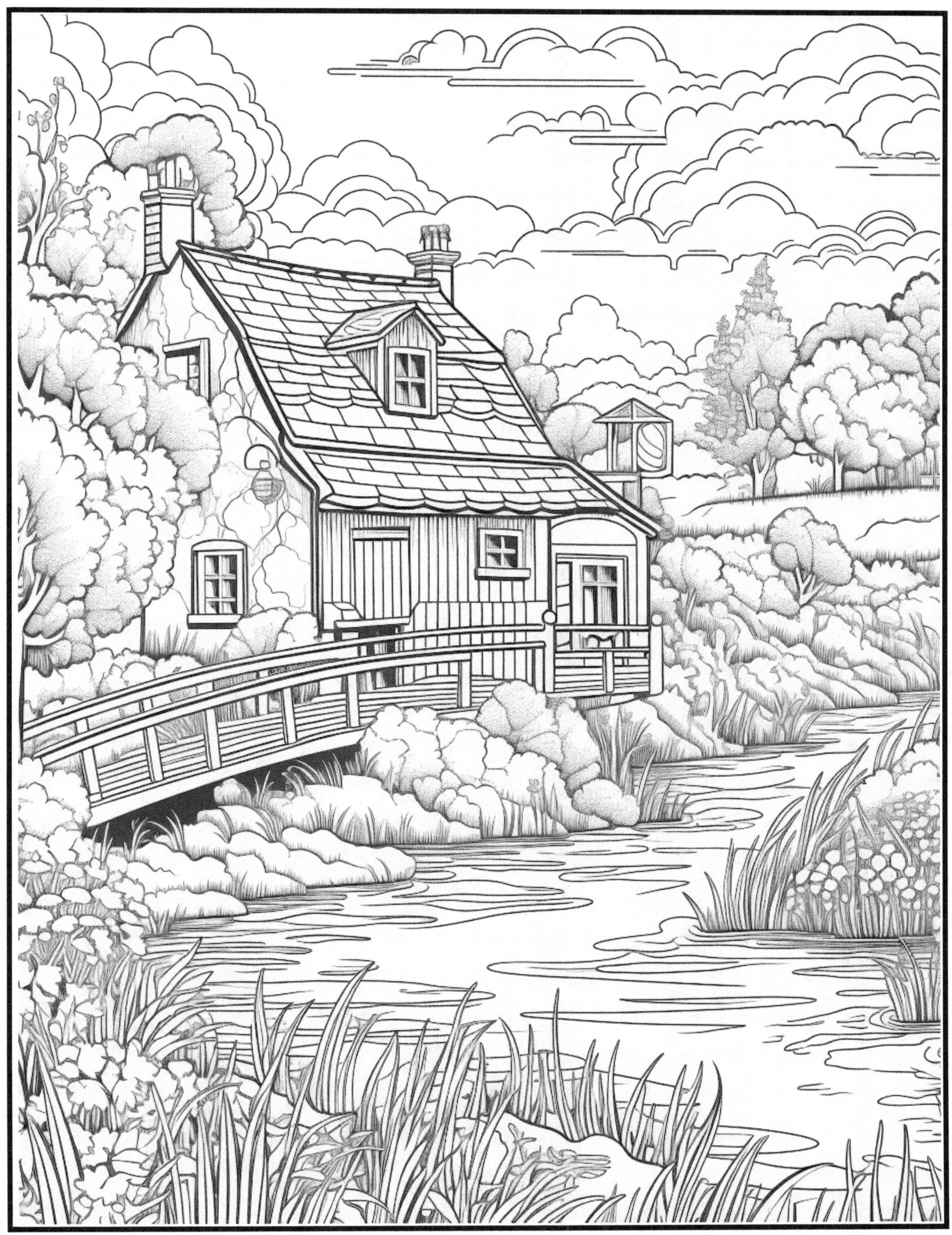

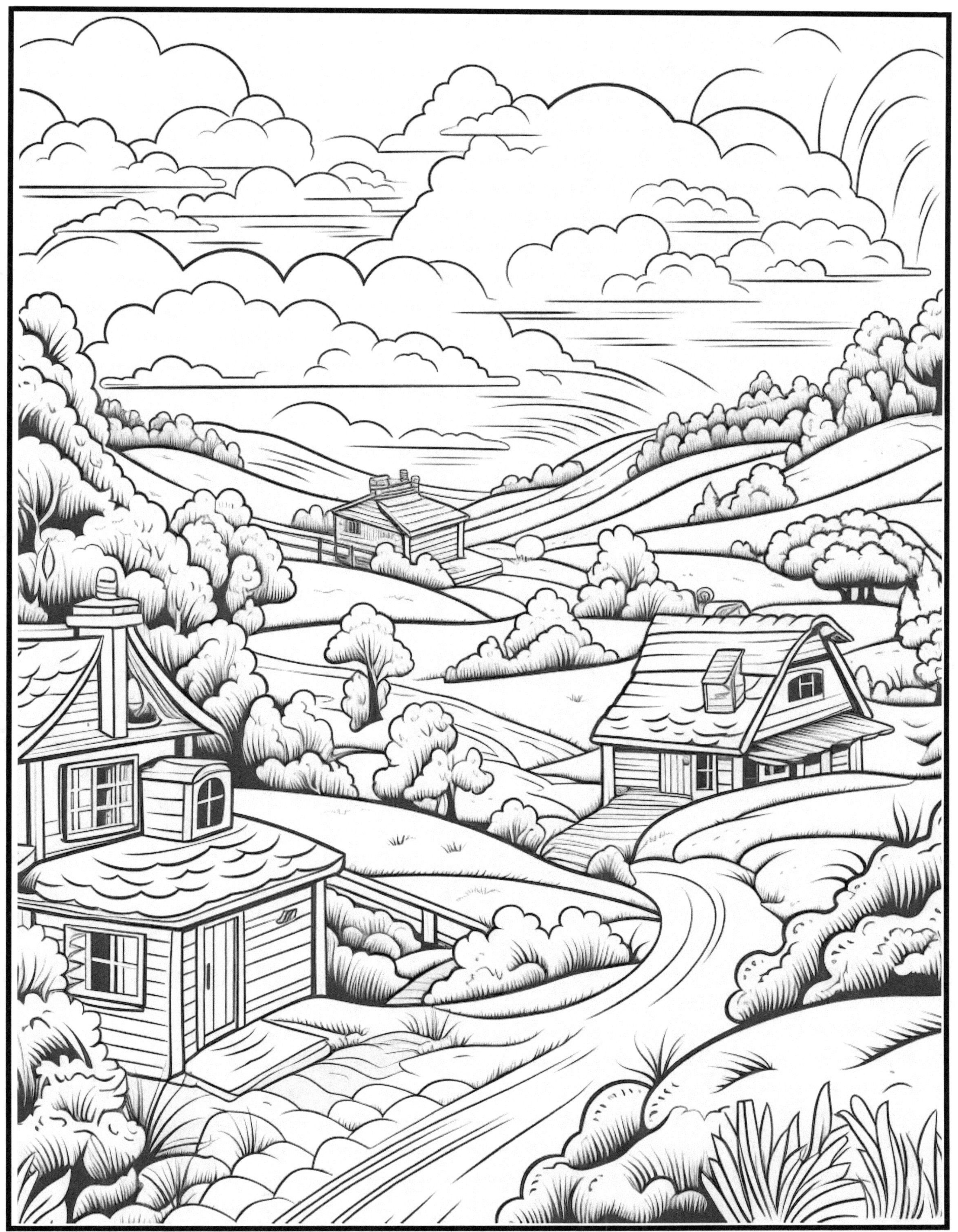

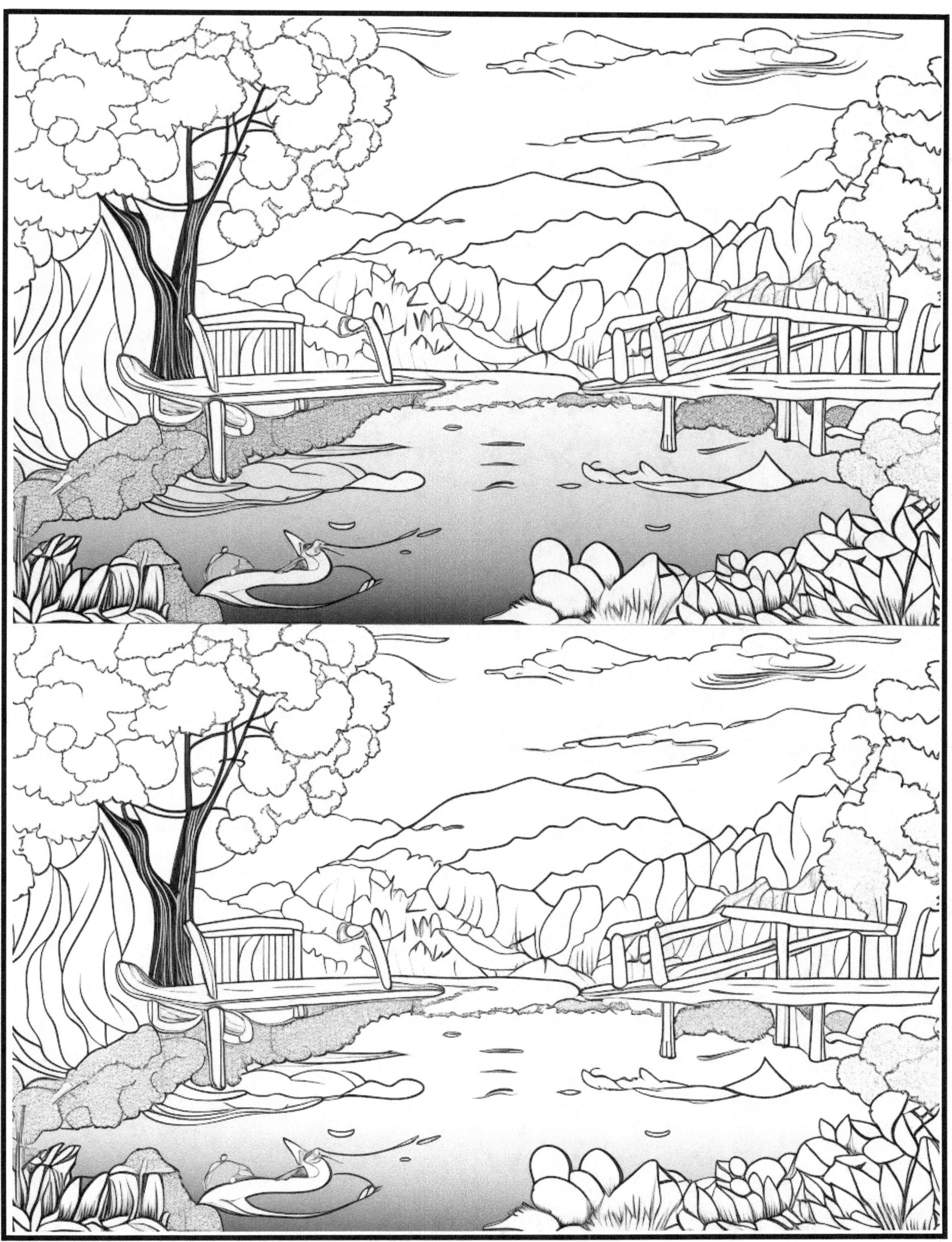

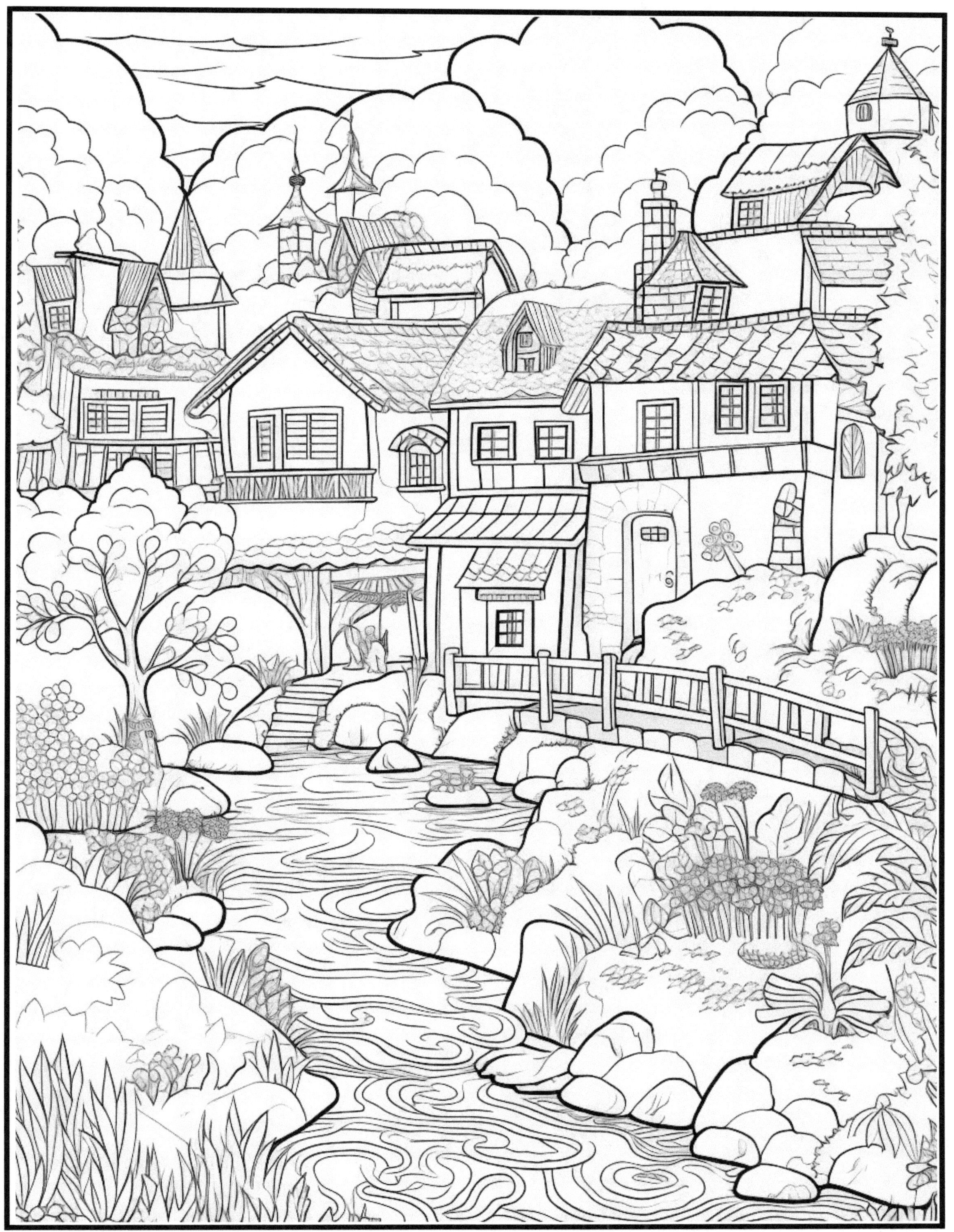

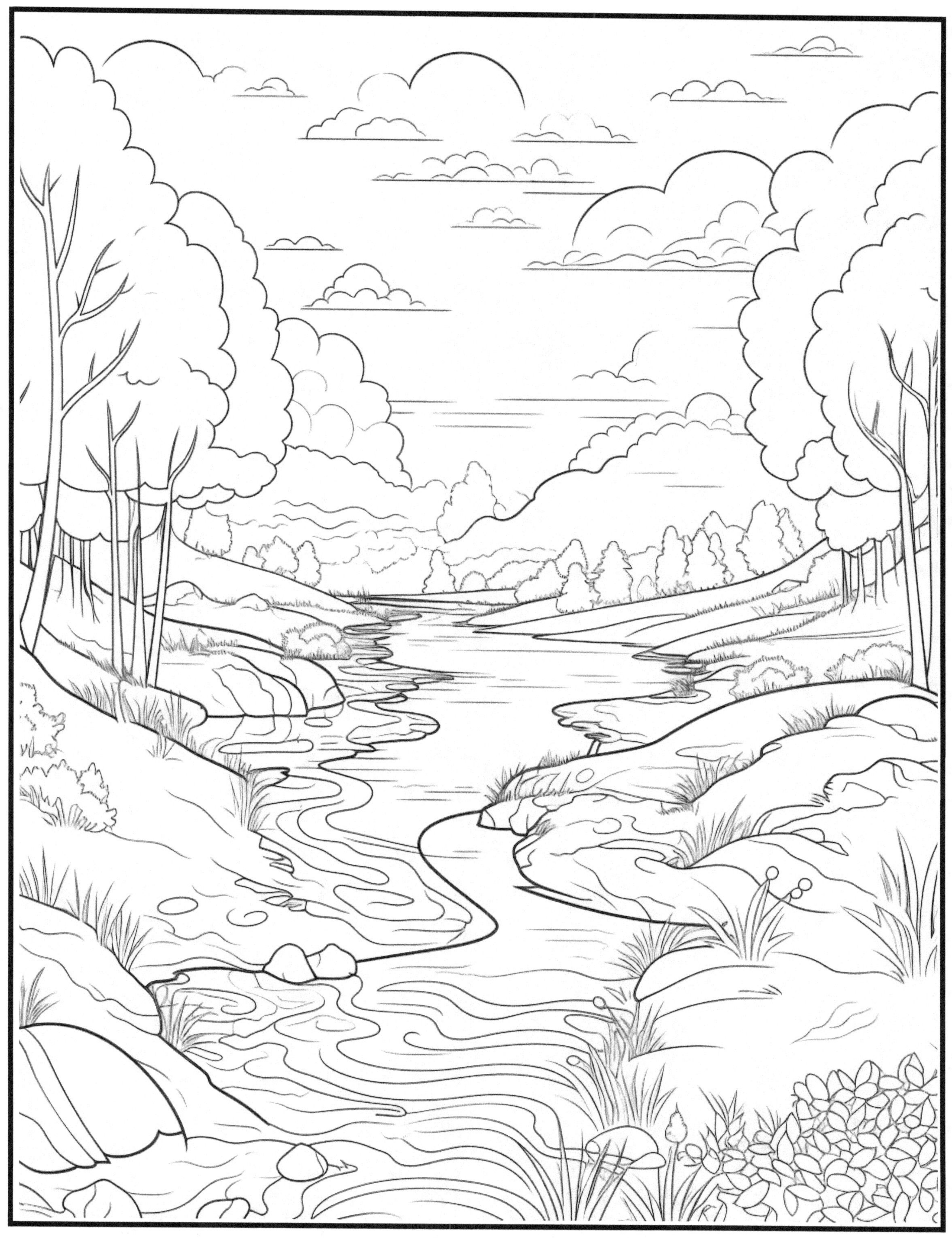

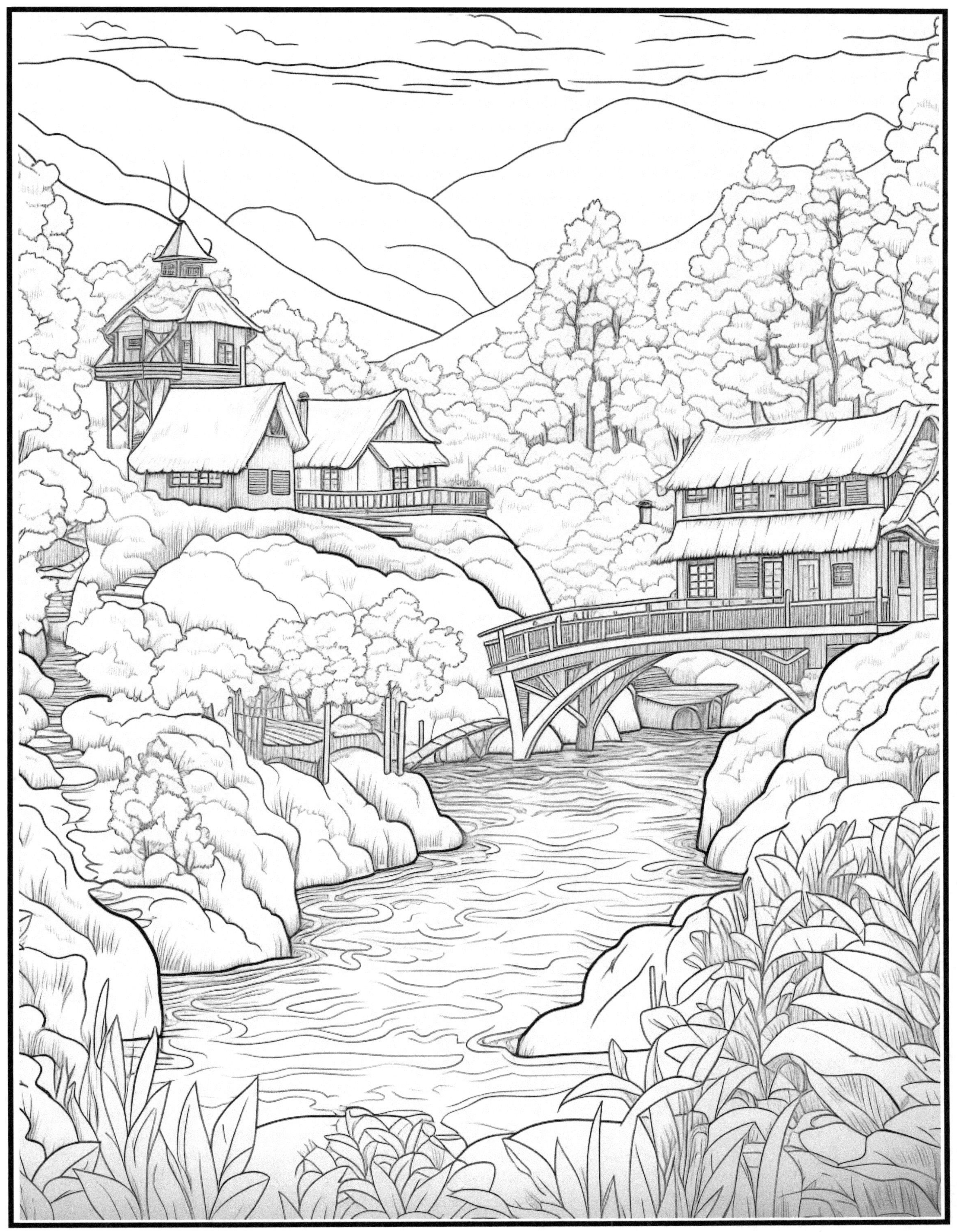

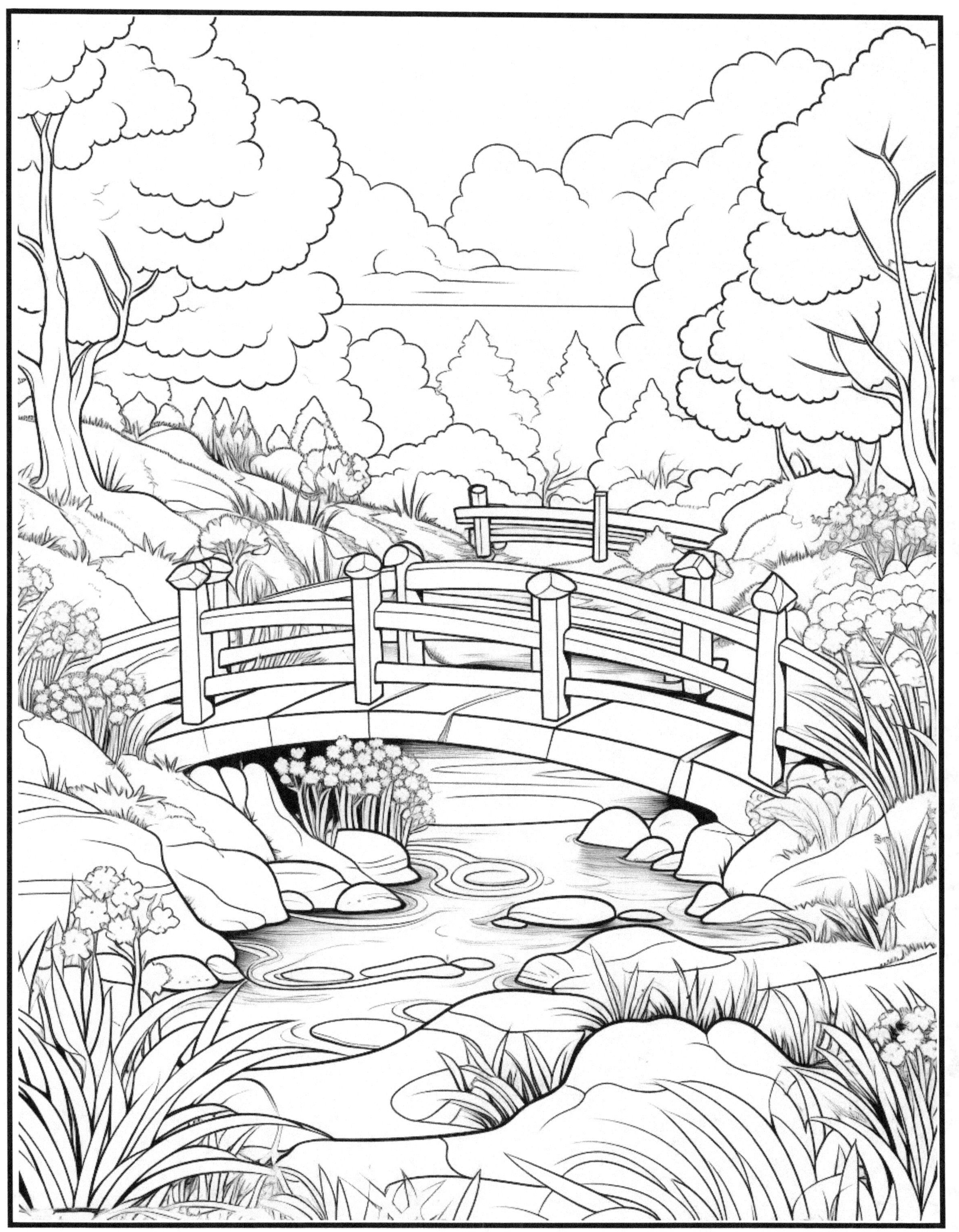

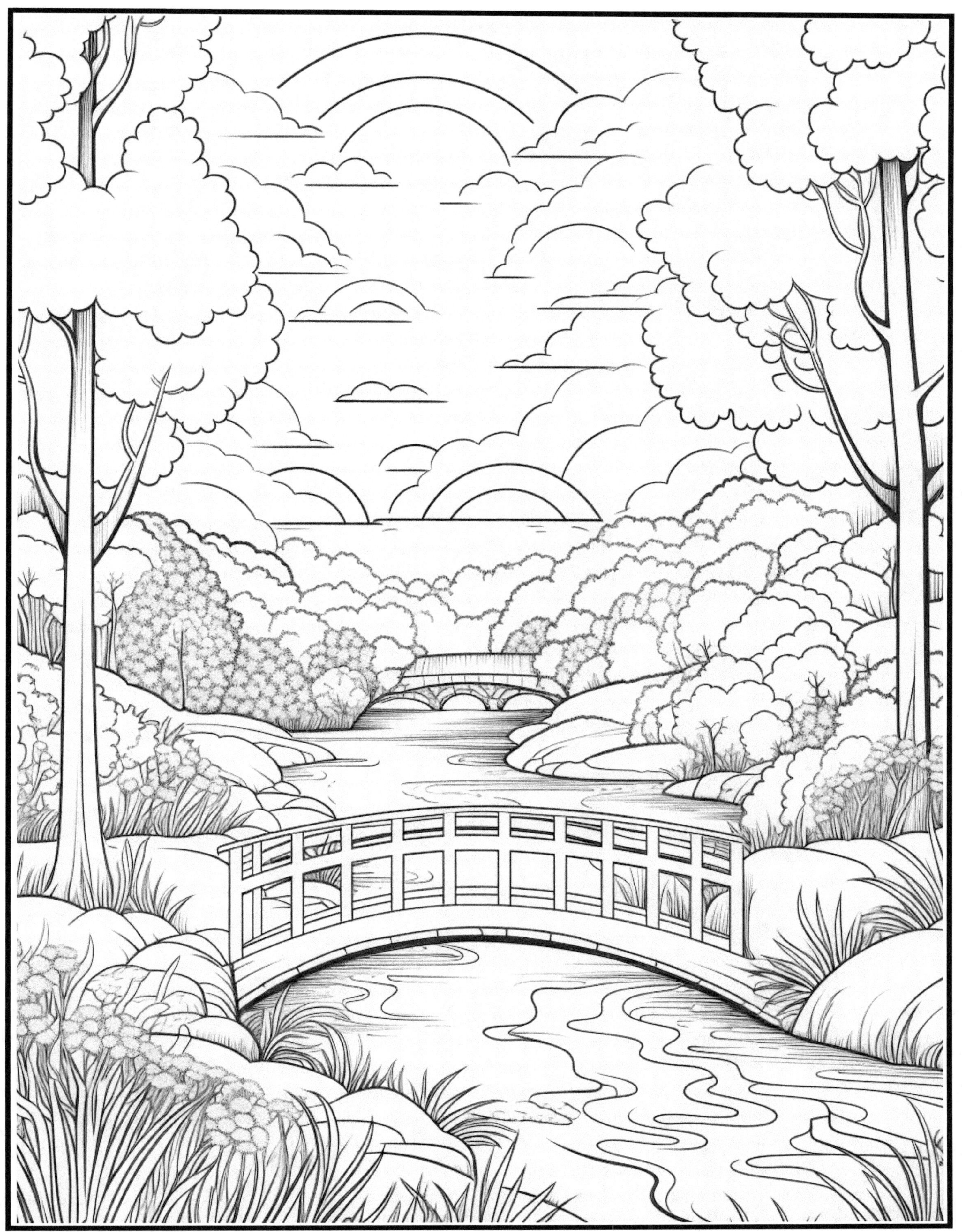

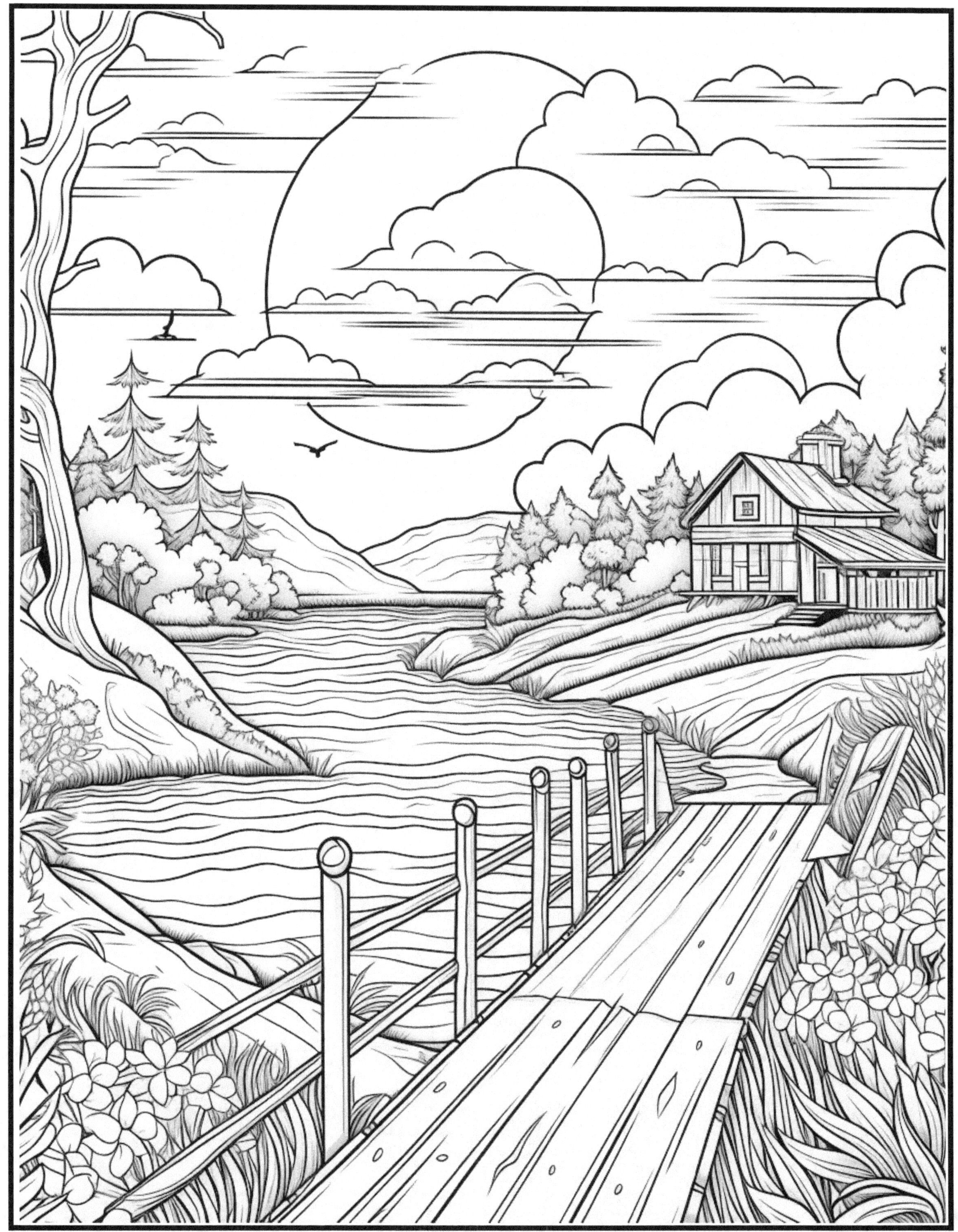

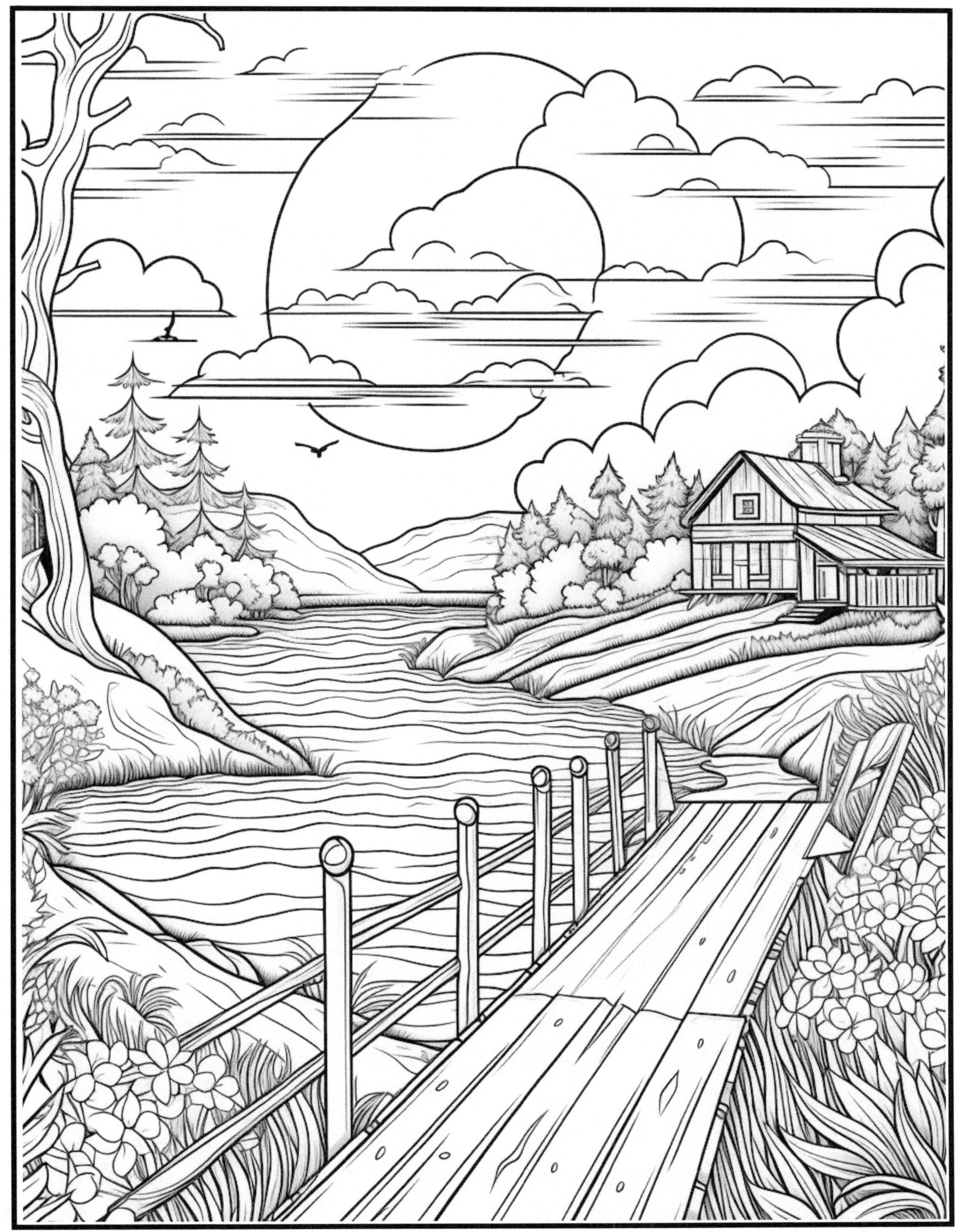

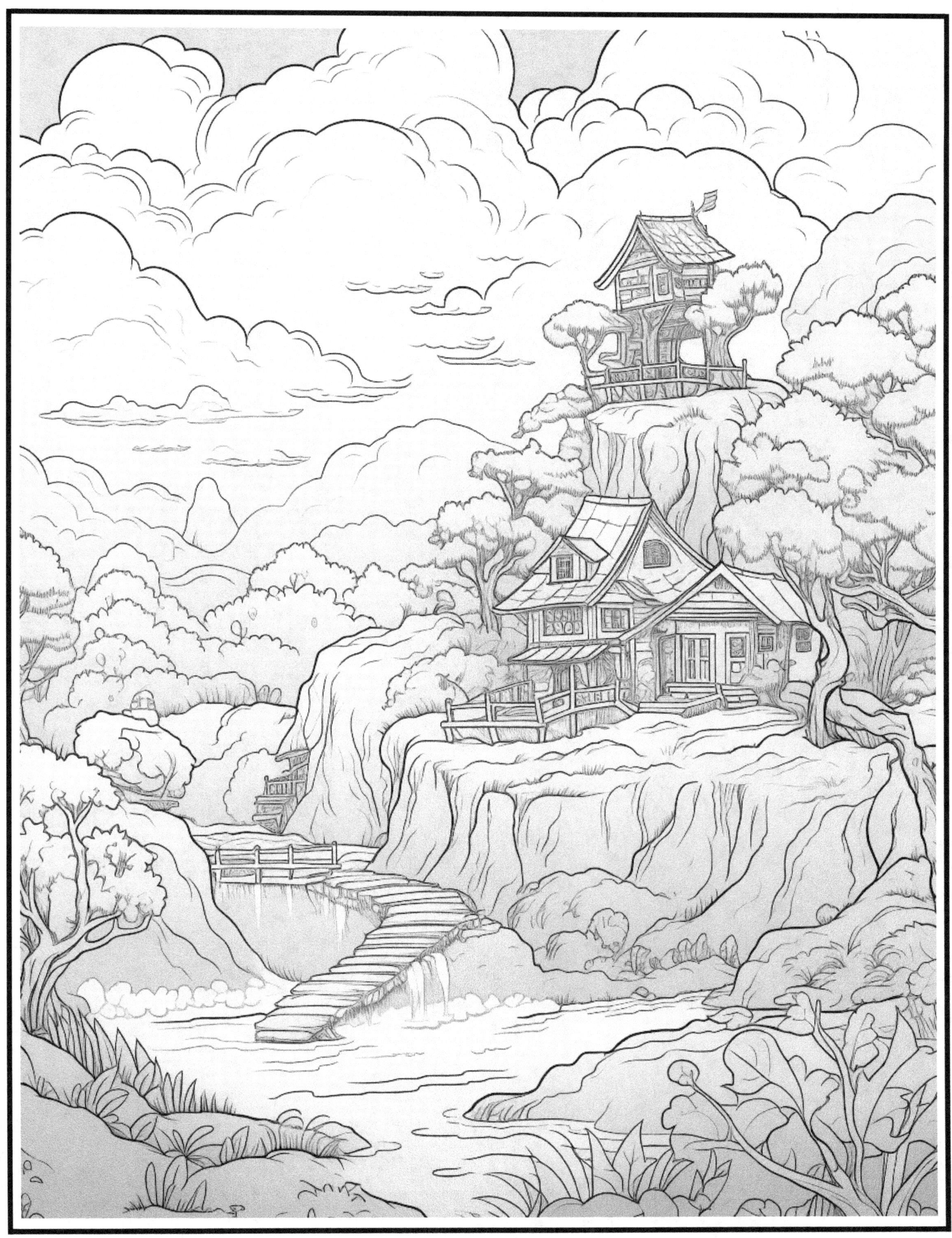

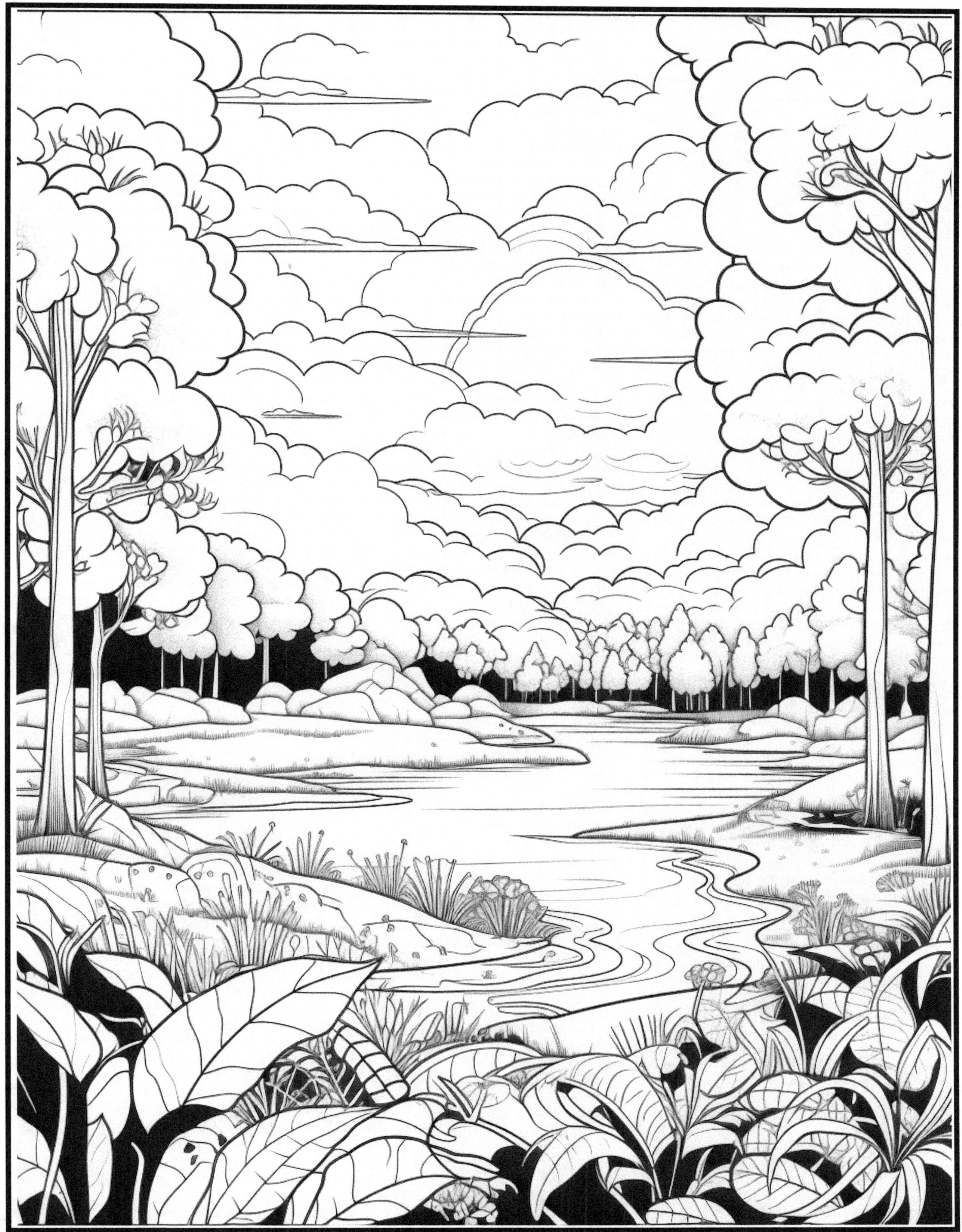

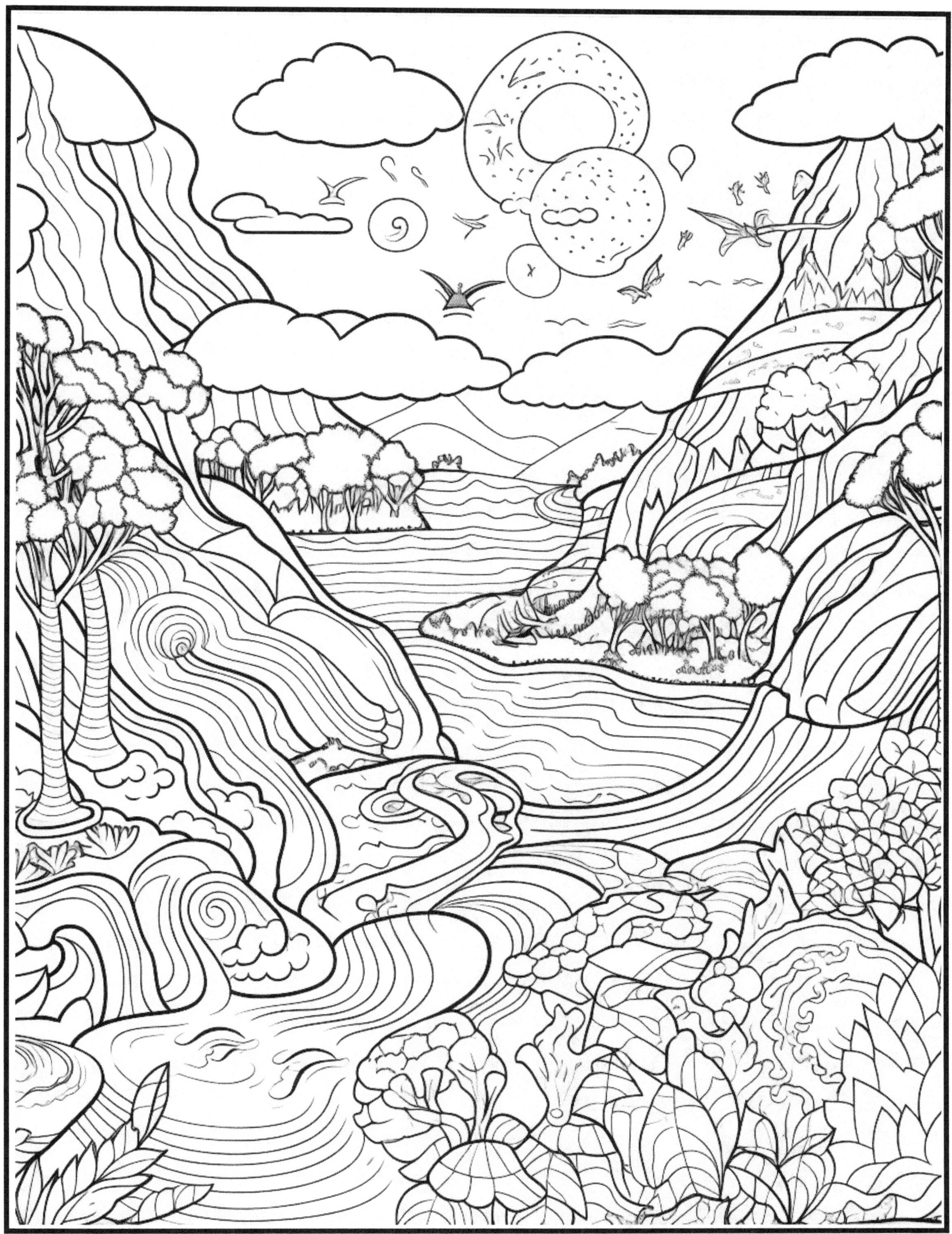

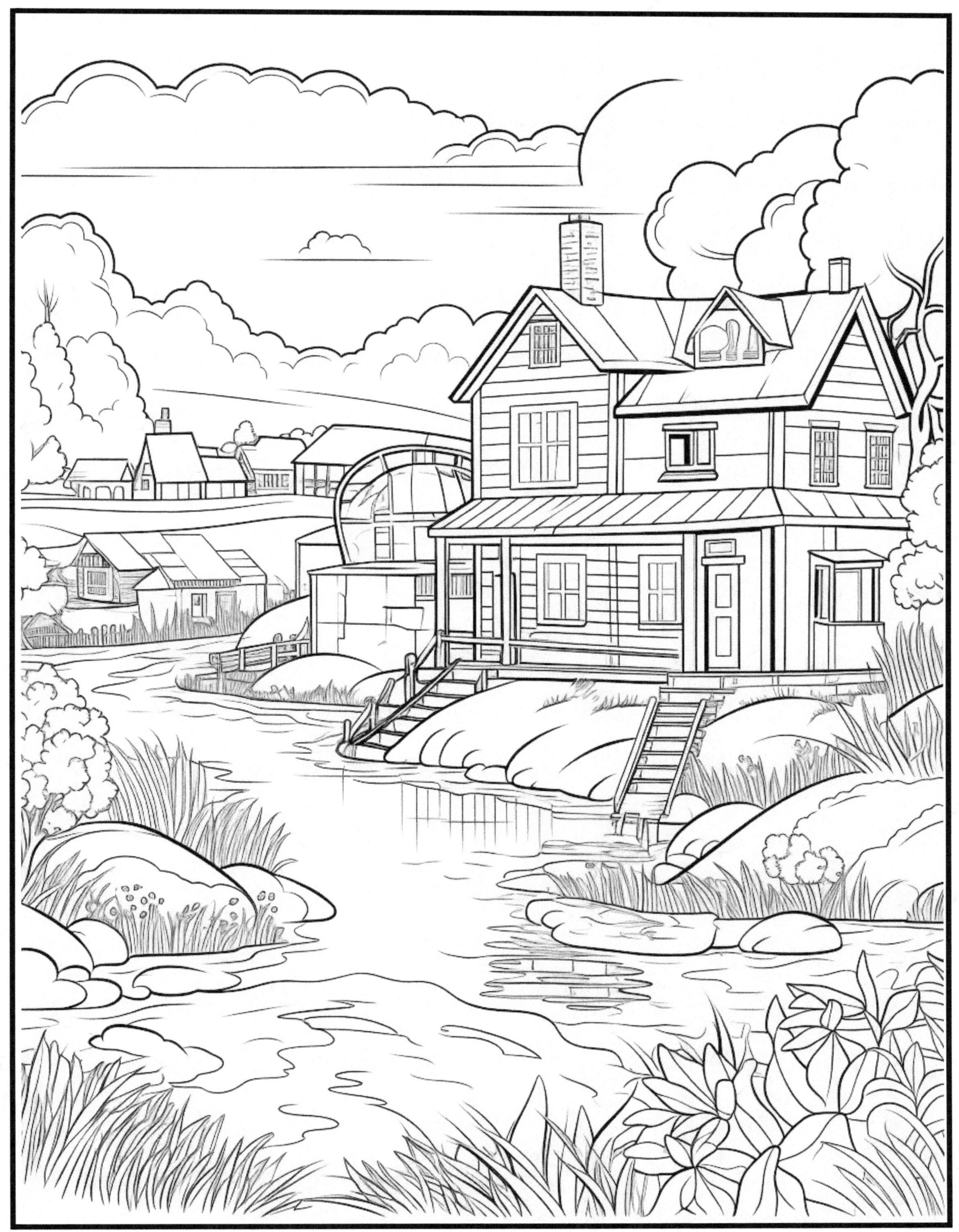

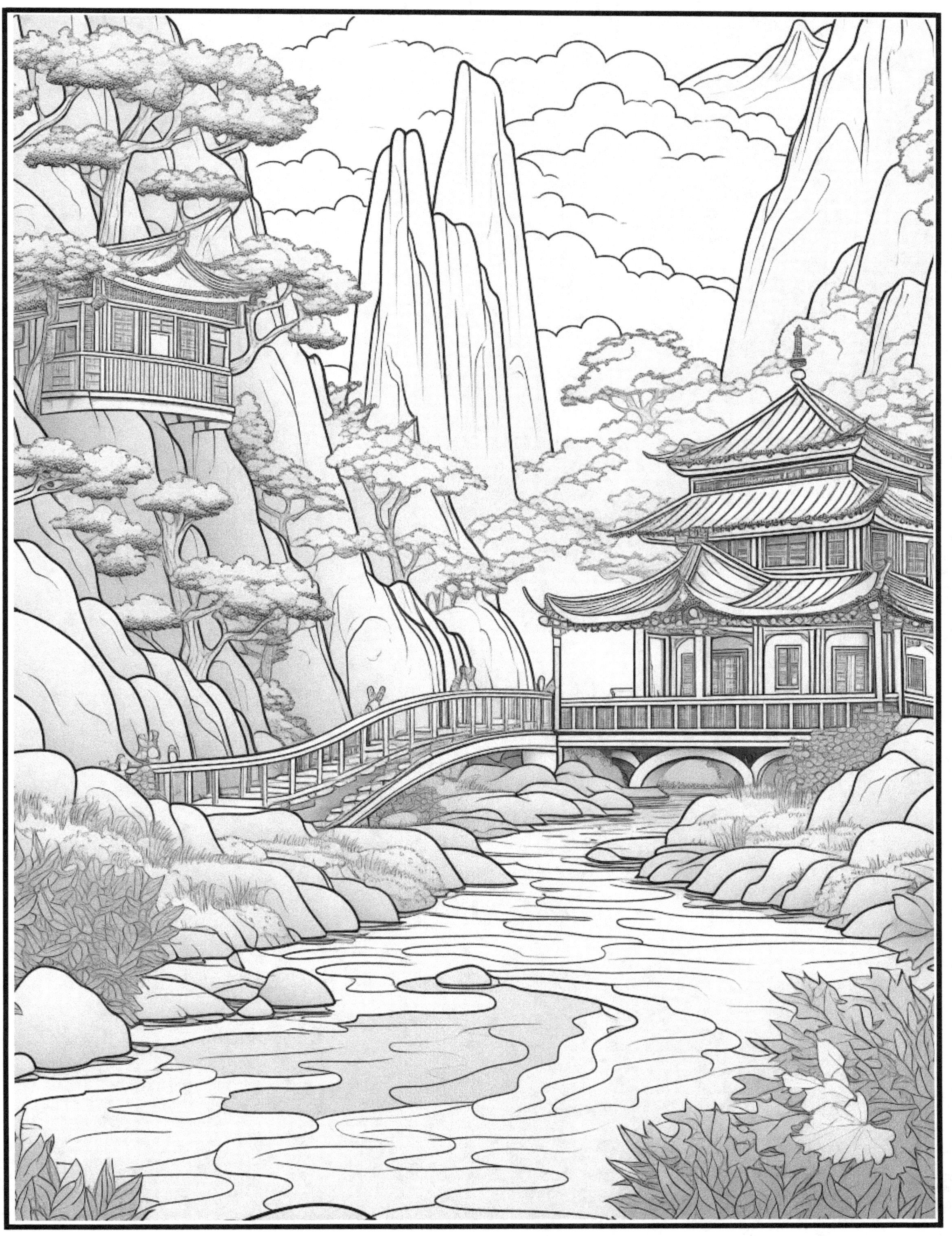

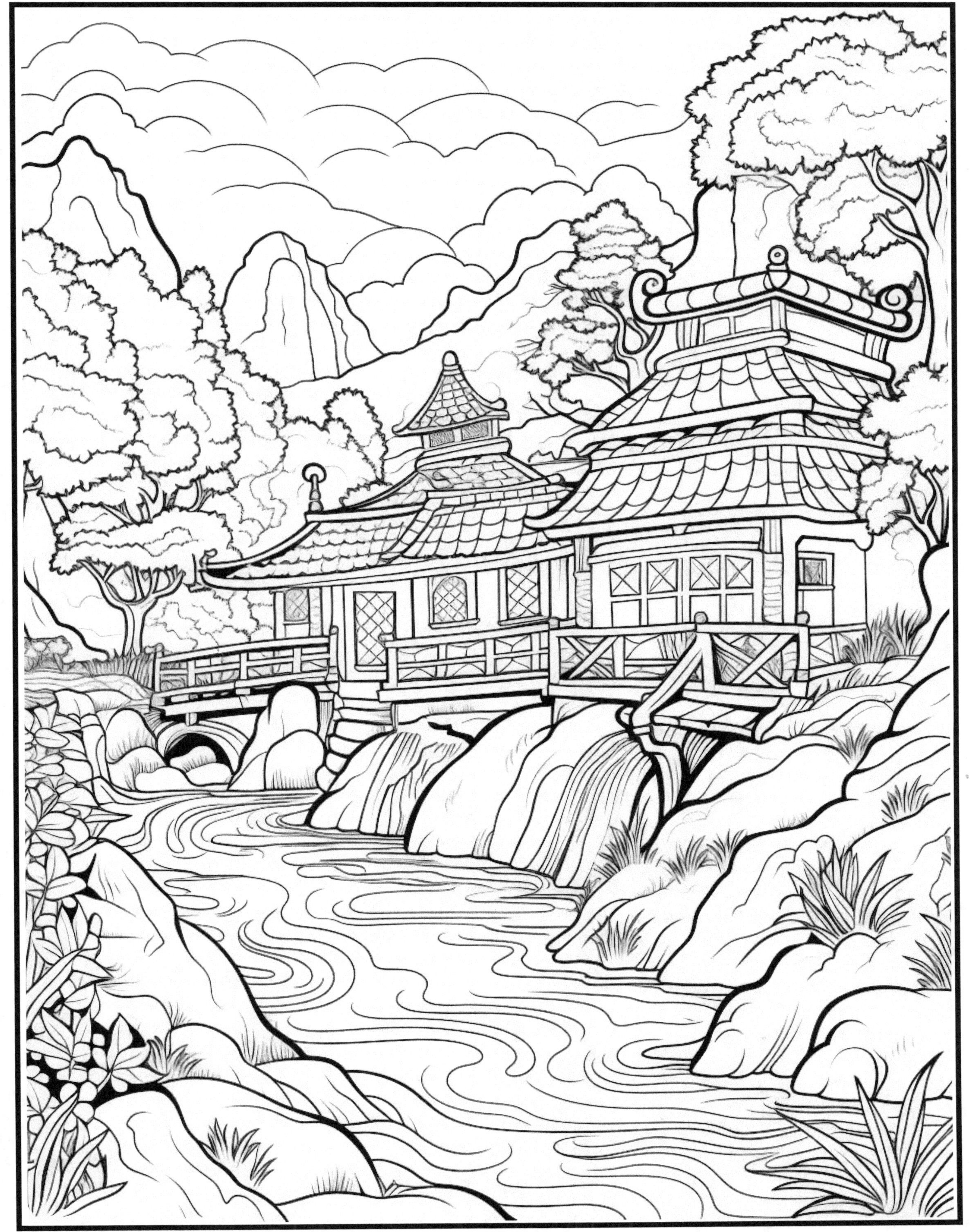

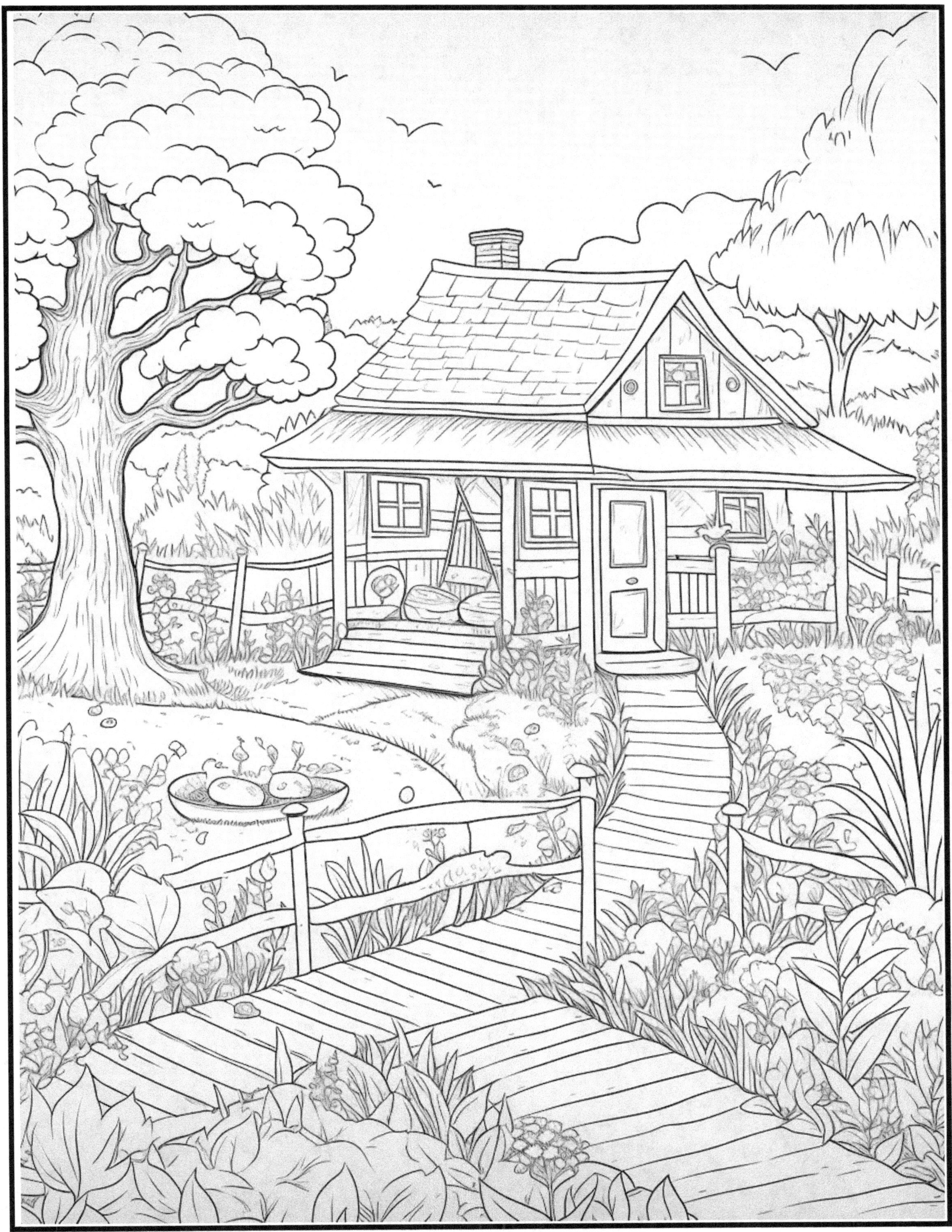

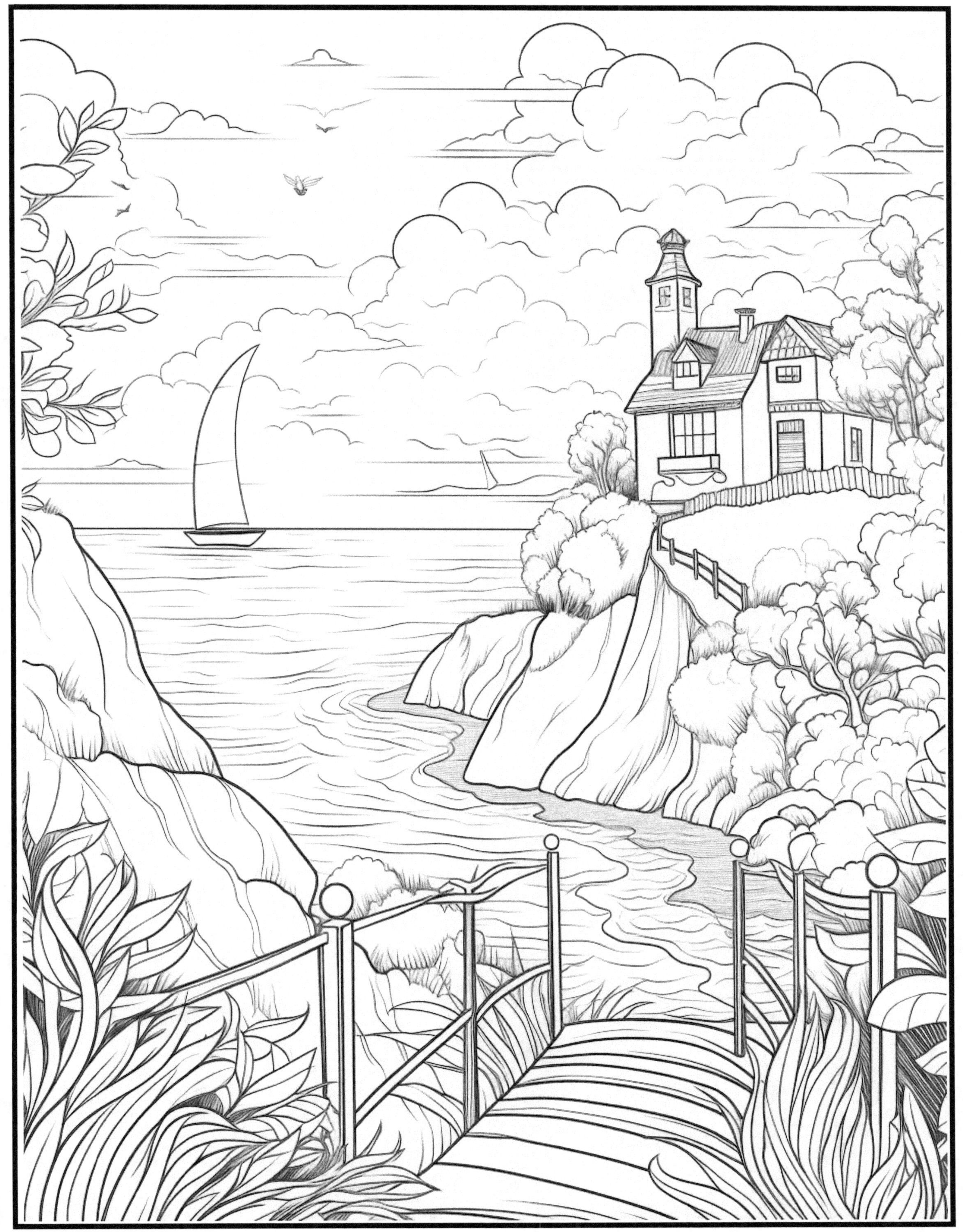

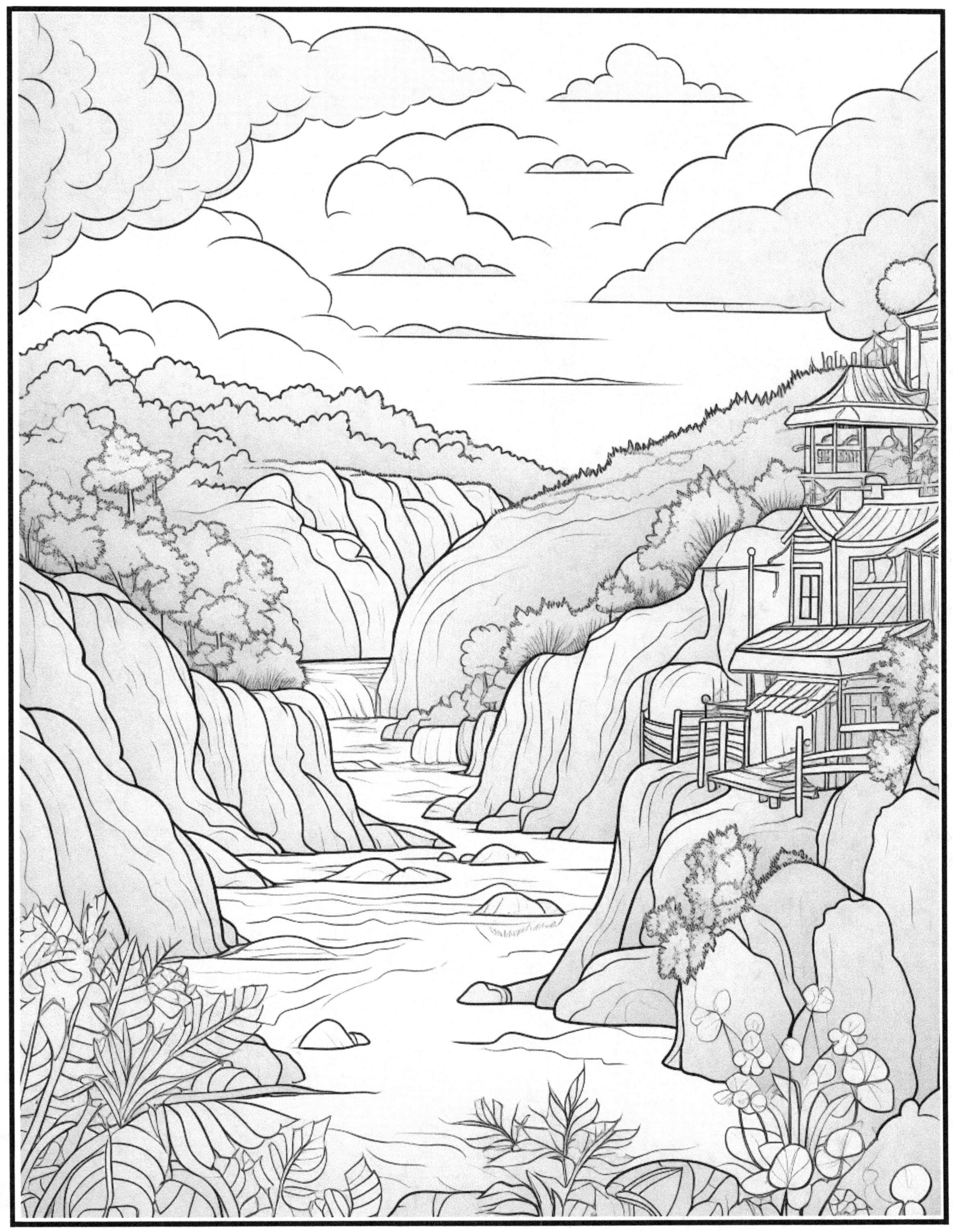

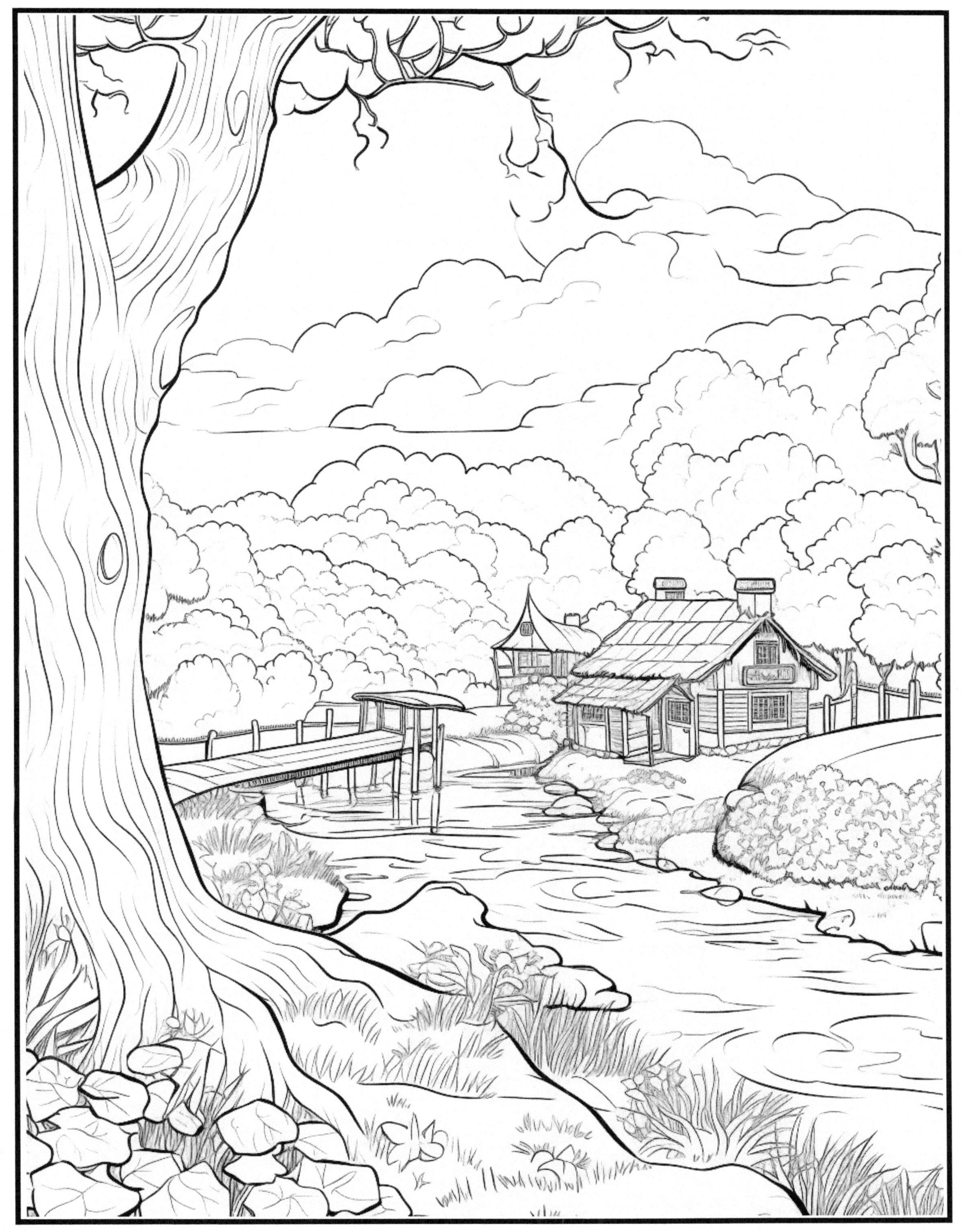

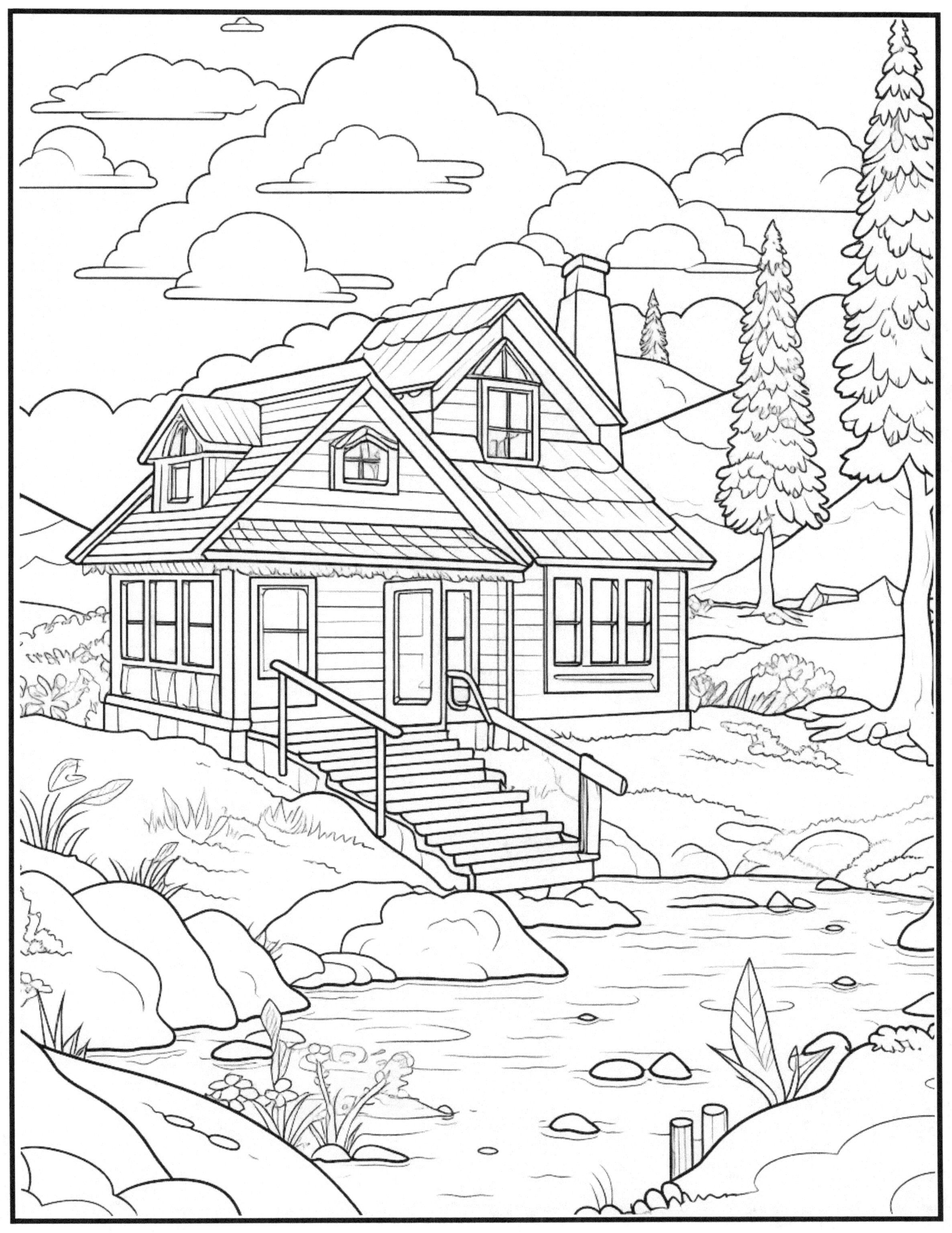

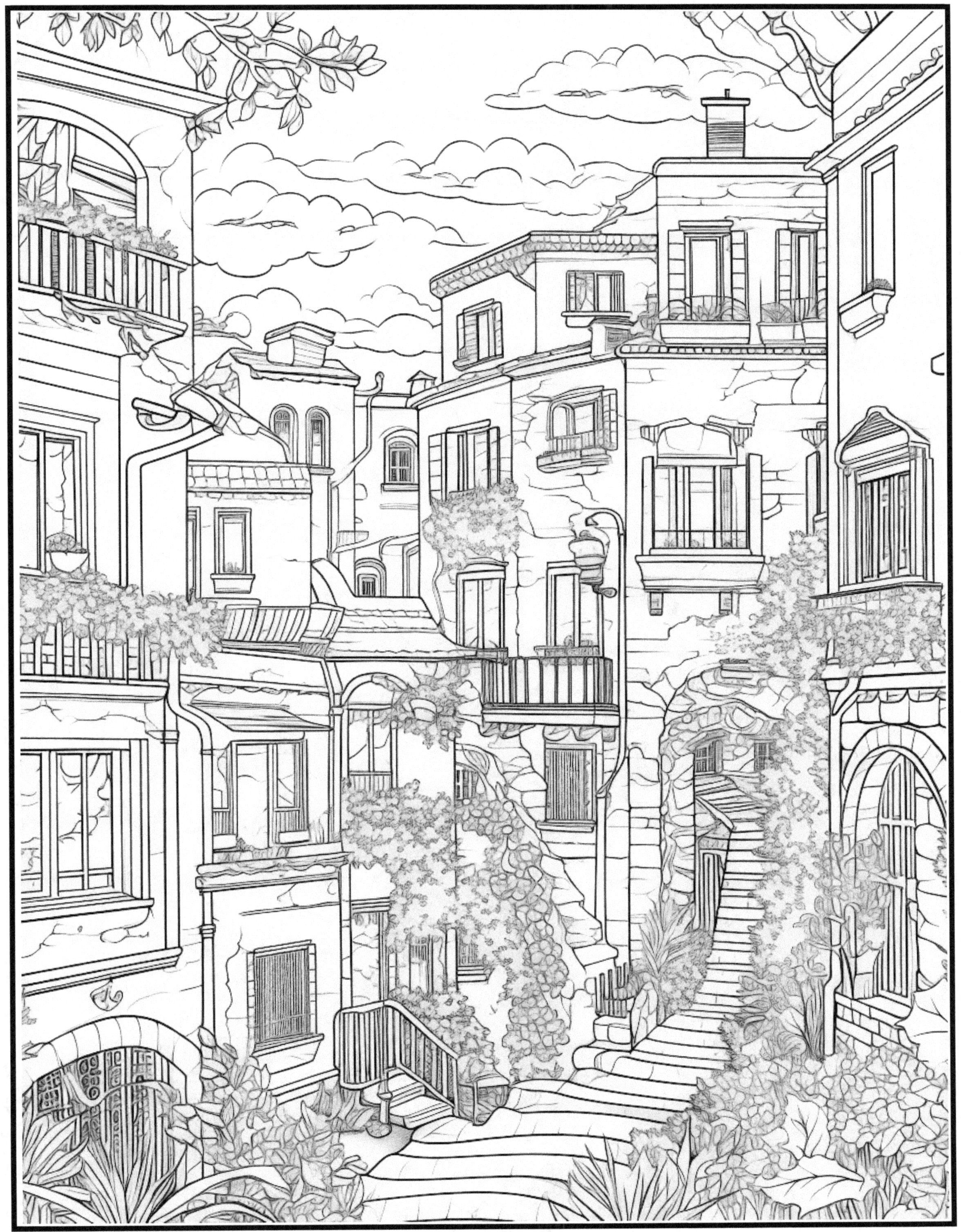

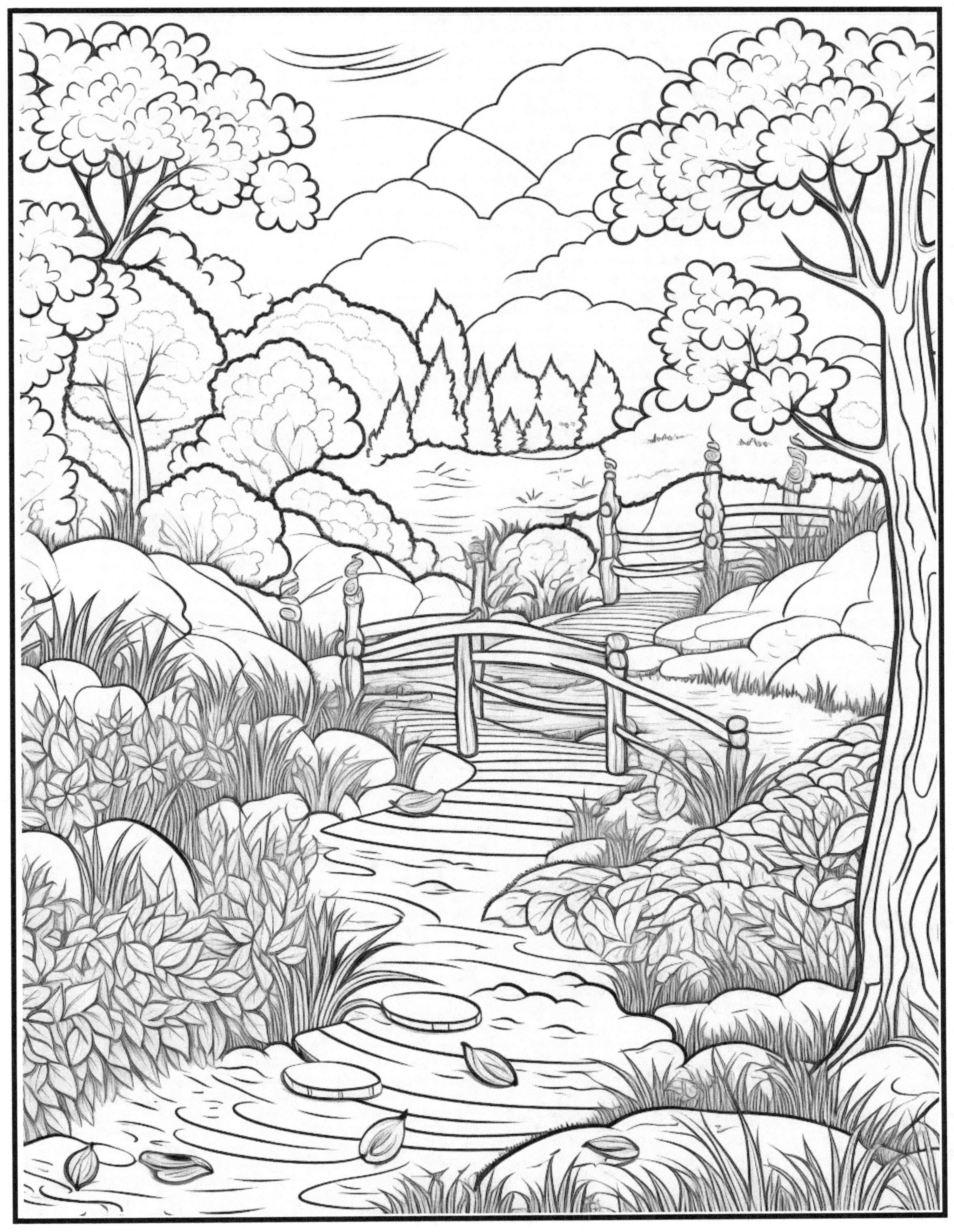

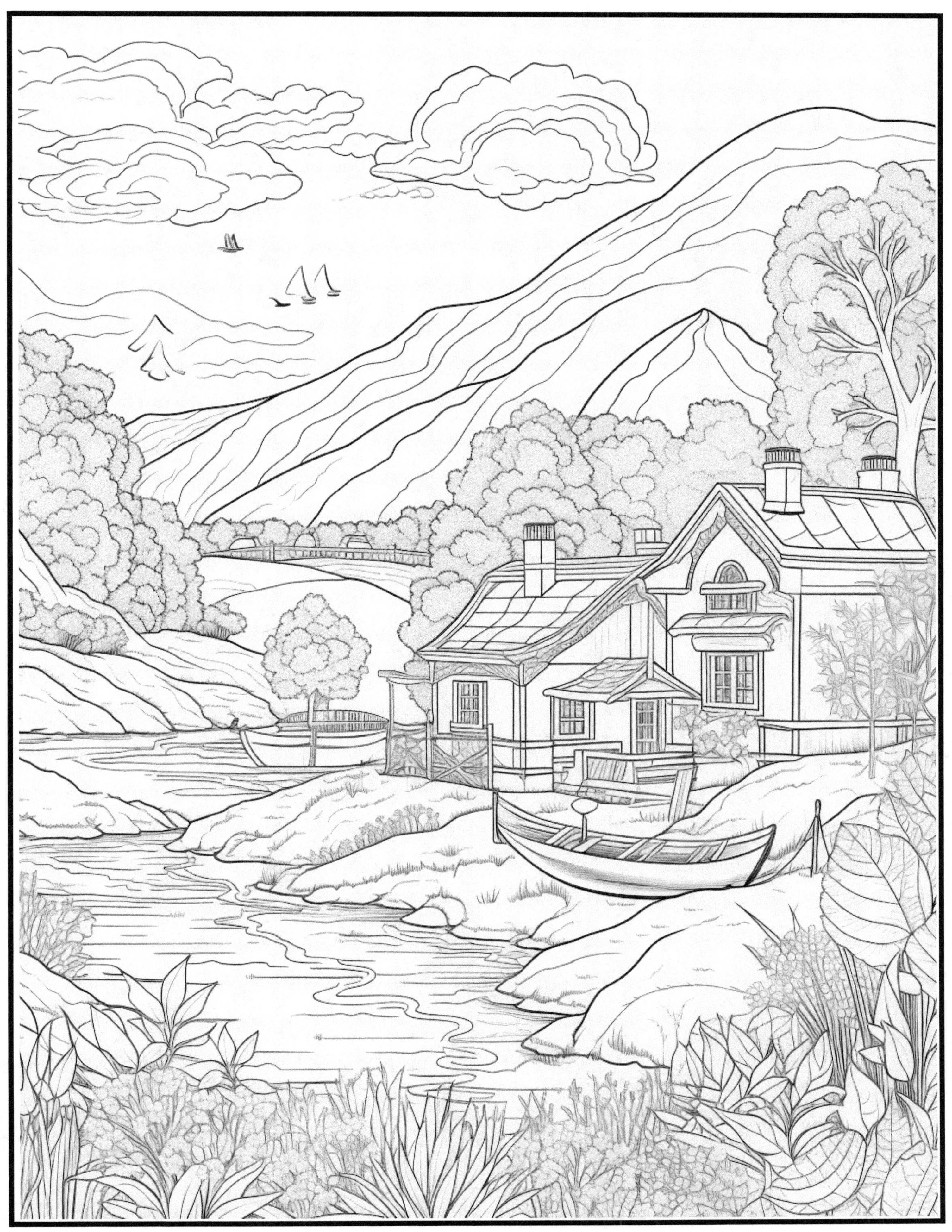

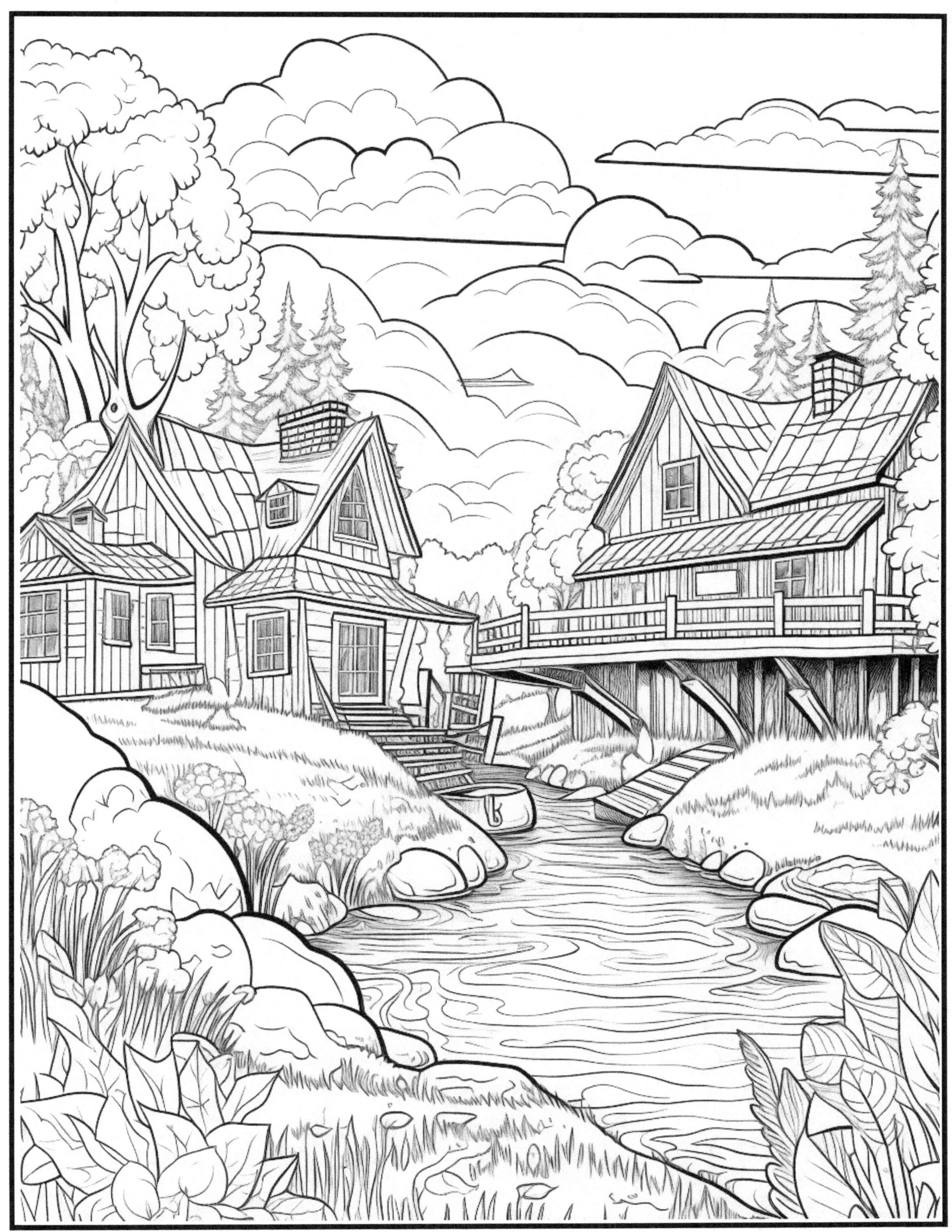

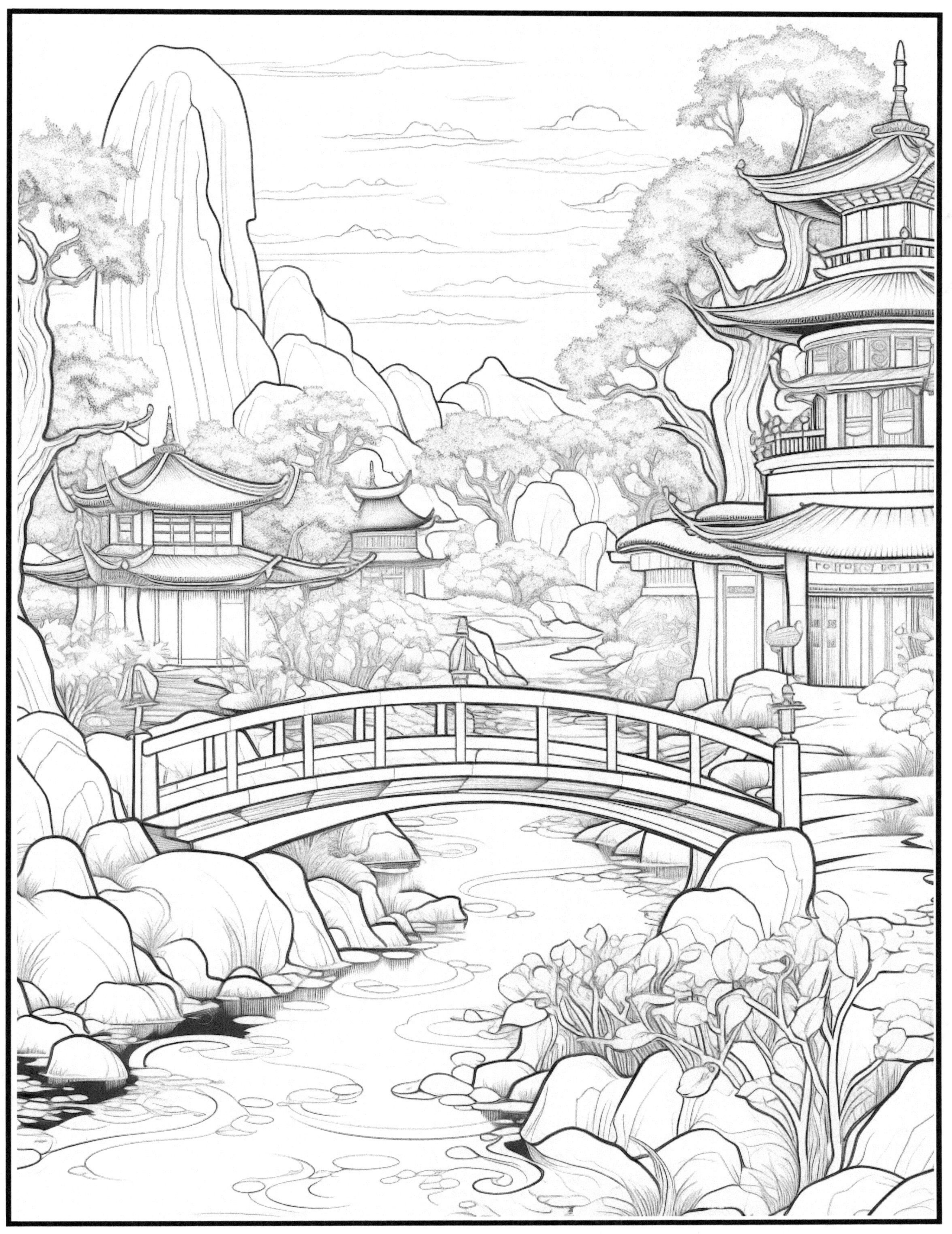

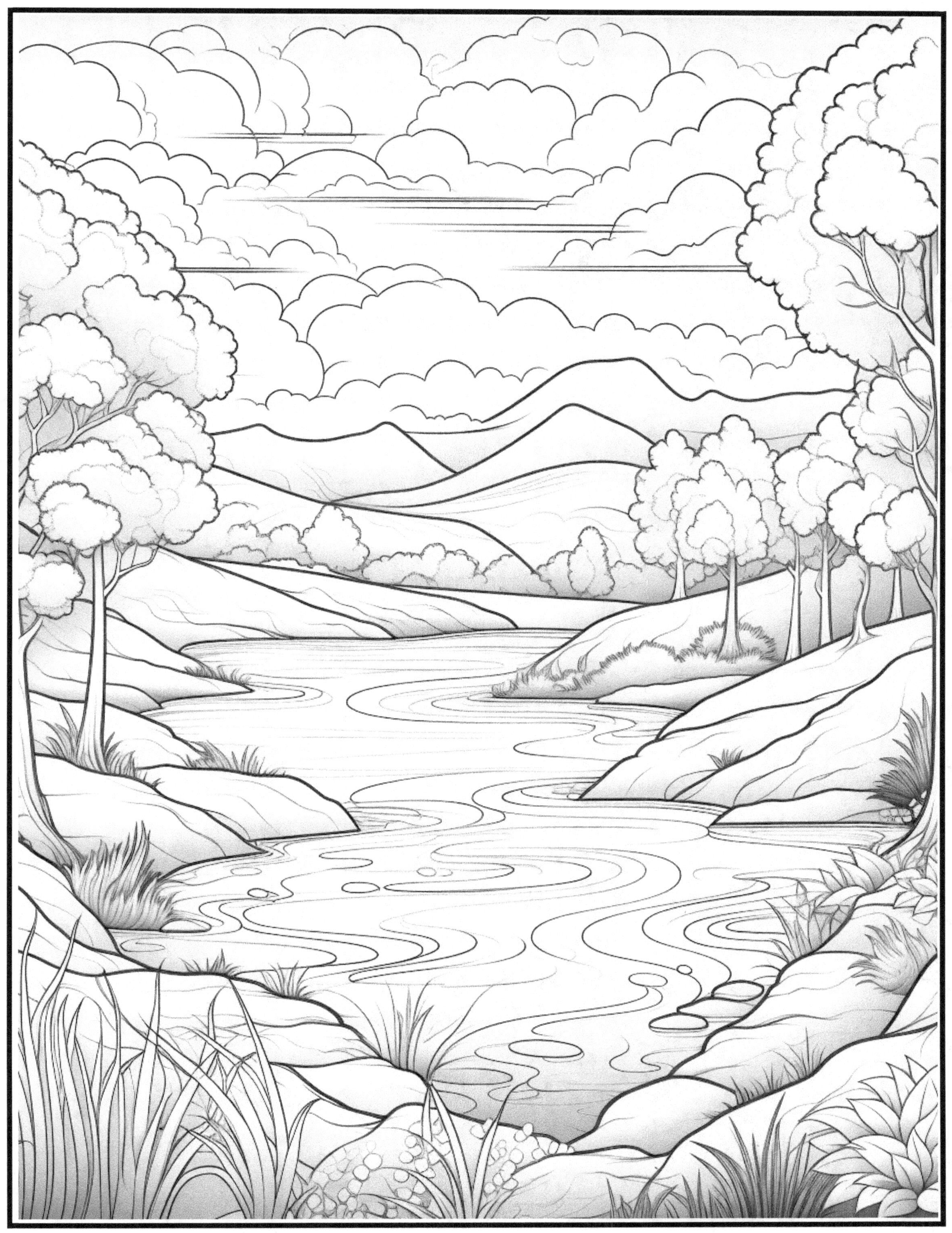

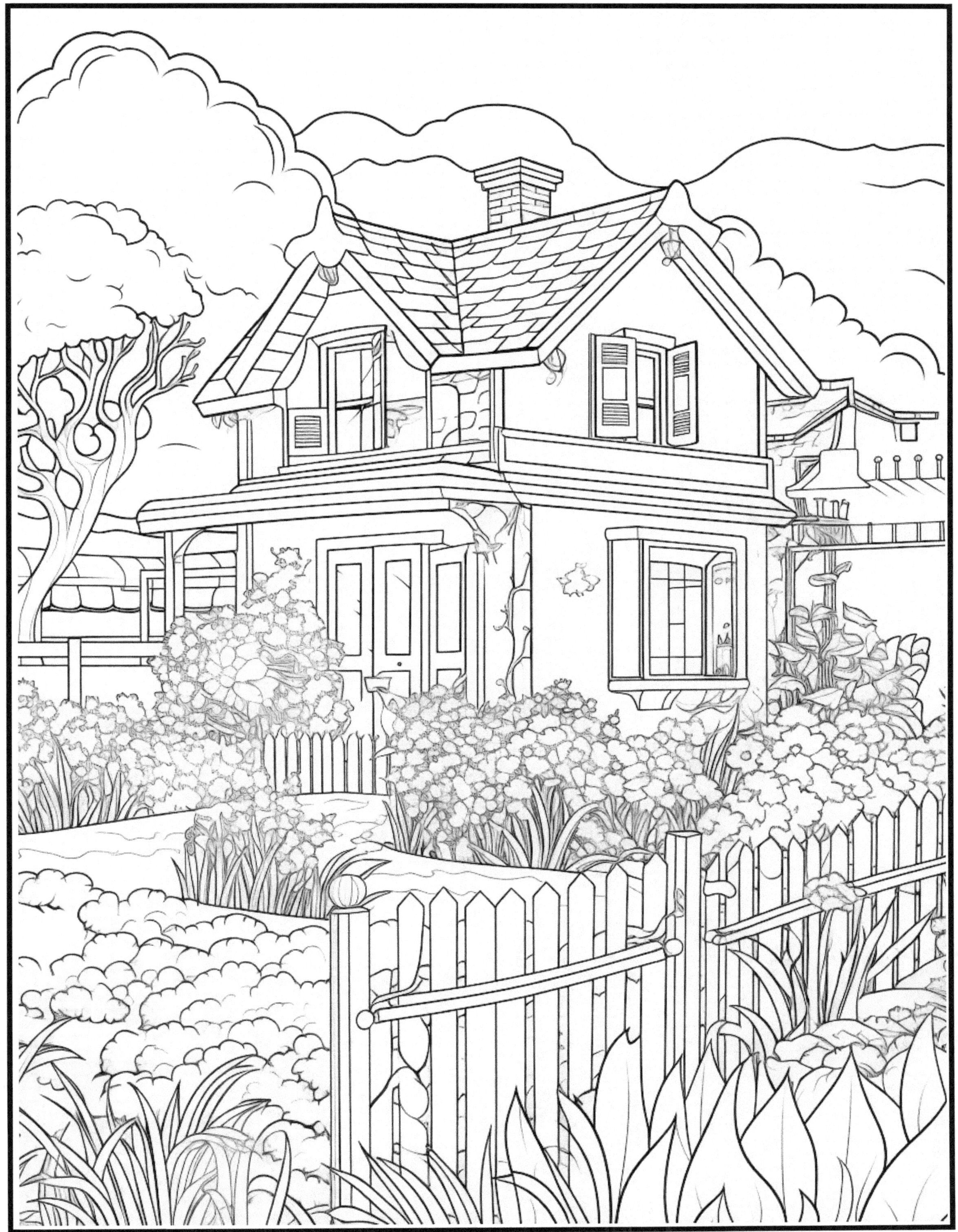

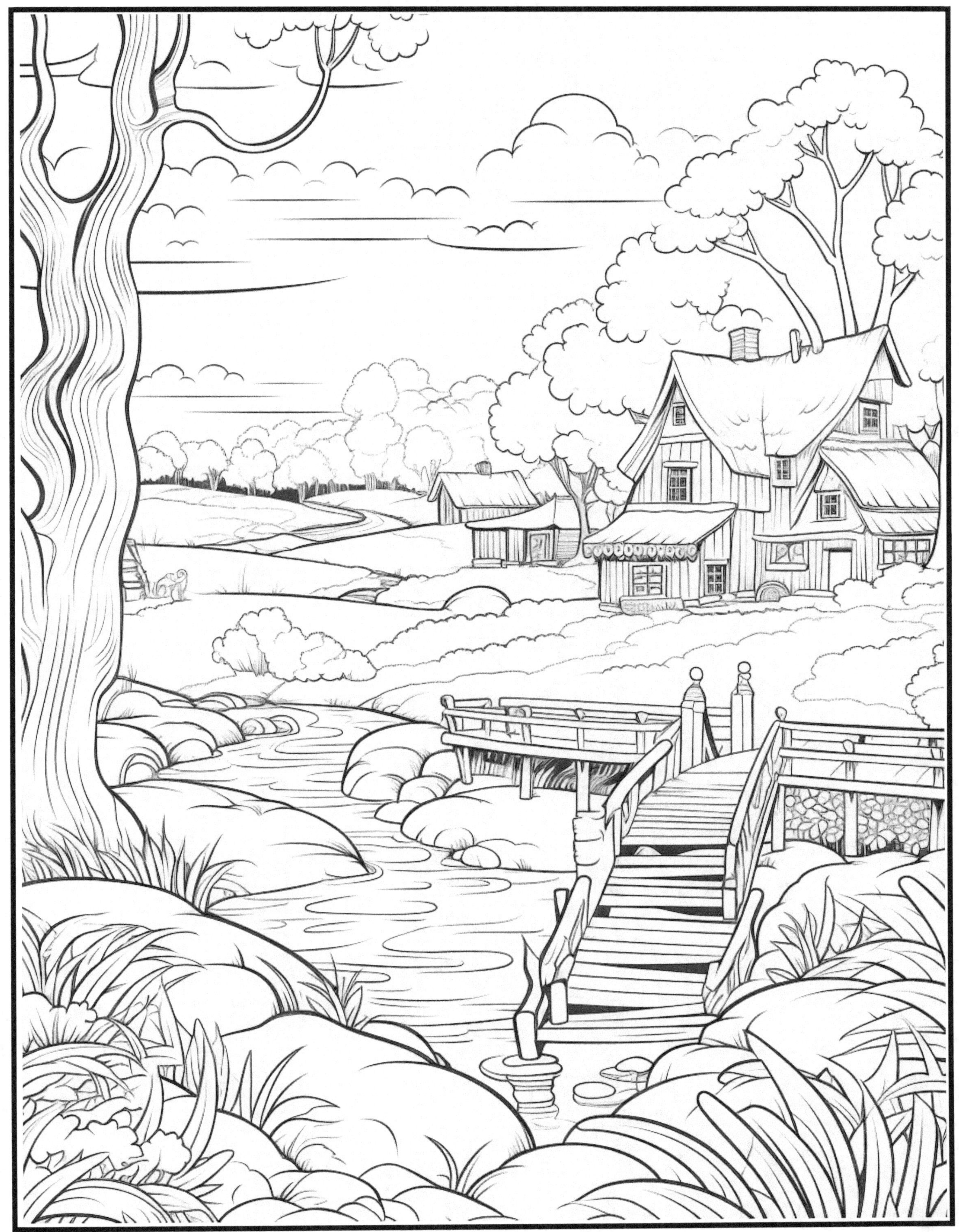

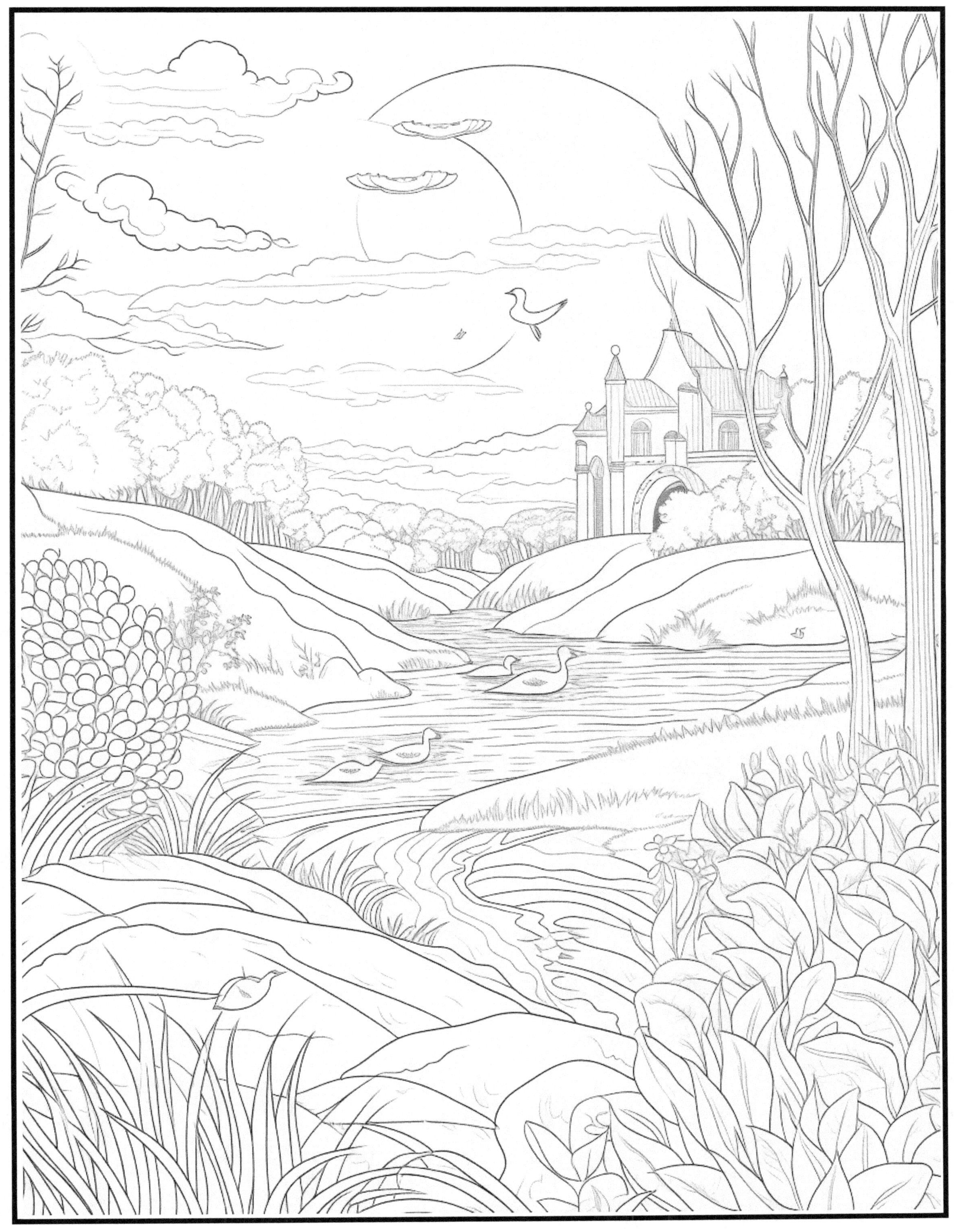

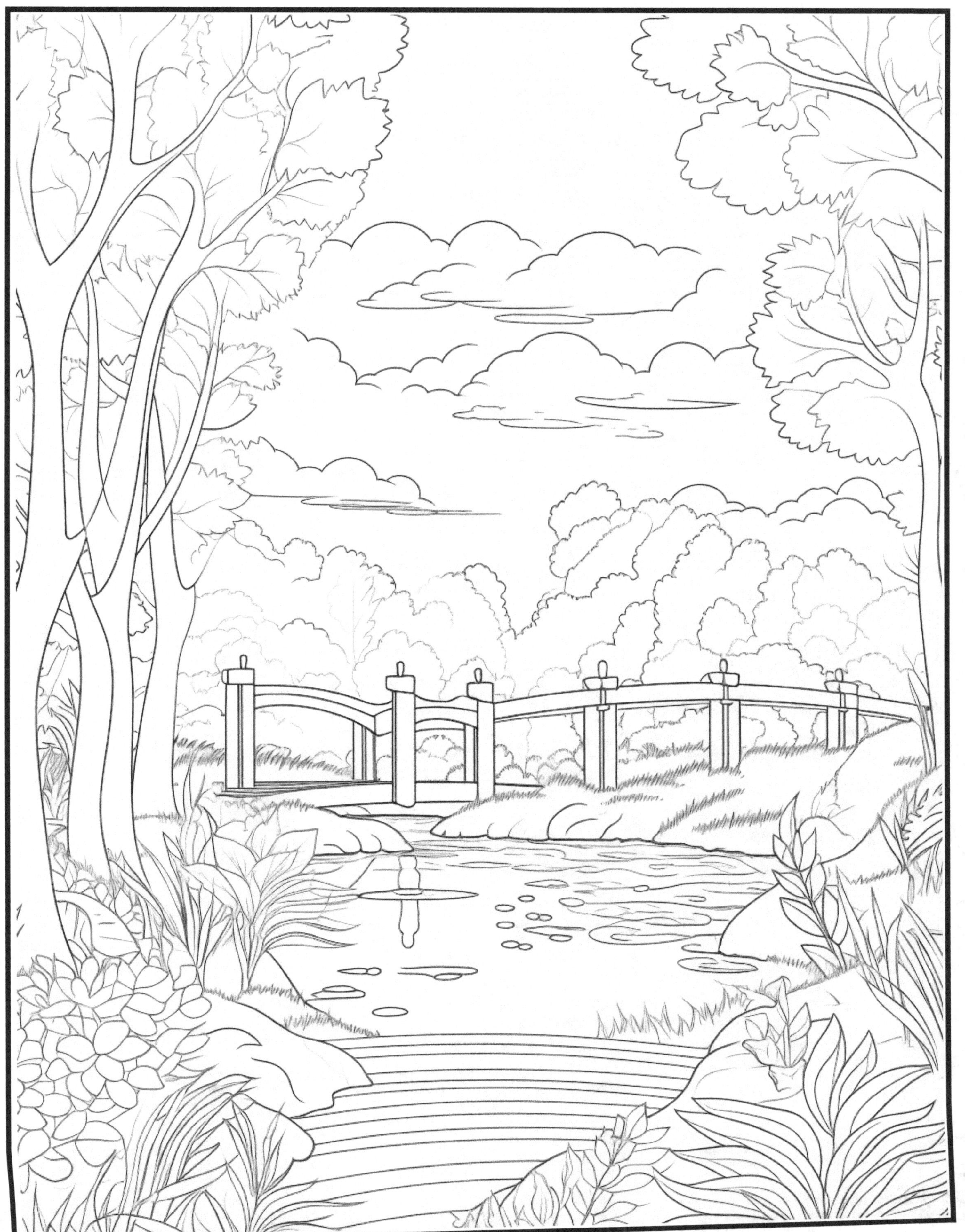